DATE DUE

French and Indian War

French and Indian War

Laurie Collier
Hillstrom and
Kevin Hillstrom

Lawrence W. Baker and
Julie L. Carnagie, Editors

U·X·L®

THOMSON

GALE

Detroit • New York • San Diego • San Francisco • Cleveland • New Haven, Conn. • Waterville, Maine • London • Munich

French and Indian War

Laurie Collier Hillstrom and Kevin Hillstrom

Project Editors
Lawrence W. Baker, Julie L. Carnagie

Permissions
Margaret Chamberlain

Imaging and Multimedia
Leitha Etheridge-Sims, Mary Grimes, Lezlie Light, Dan Newell, Christine O'Bryan, Robyn Young

Product Design
Pamela A. E. Galbreath

Composition
Evi Seoud

Manufacturing
Rita Wimberley

LIBRARY OF CONGRESS CATALOG CARD NUMBER

Hillstrom, Laurie Collier, 1965–
    French and Indian War / Laurie Collier Hillstrom and Kevin Hillstrom ; Lawrence W. Baker and Julie L. Carnagie, editors.
        p. cm.
    Summary: A comprehensive overview of the French and Indian War, including bi-ographies and full or excerpted memoirs, speeches, and other source documents. Includes bibliographical references and index.
        ISBN 0-7876-6560-6
        1. United States—History—French and Indian War, 1755–1763—Juvenile litera-ture. [1. United States—History—French and Indian War, 1755–1763.] I. Hillstrom, Kevin, 1963– II. Baker, Lawrence W. III. Carnagie, Julie. IV. Title.
        E199 .H55 2003
        973.2'6—dc21
                                                            2002155415

Printed in the United States of America
10 9 8 7 6 5 4 3 2 1

Contents

Almanac

Biographies

Reader's Guide

French and Indian War presents a comprehensive overview of the struggle for control of North America that took place between French and British forces—as well as each side's colonists and Indian allies—from 1754 to 1763. The volume is divided into two sections: Almanac and Biographies. The Almanac section consists of nine chapters that are arranged chronologically and cover all aspects of the conflict. The Almanac begins by describing the early struggles between French and British settlers for control of trade and territory in North America. It then details the progress of the war, culminating with the pivotal British victory in the Battle of Quebec. It concludes with a discussion of the enduring changes the war produced in the relationship between Great Britain and its colonies—changes that eventually led to the American Revolution (1775–83). Each chapter of the Almanac section includes "Words to Know" and "People to Know" boxes that define important terms and individuals discussed in the chapter for easy reference.

The Biographies section includes profiles of eleven important figures from the French and Indian War era. The essays cover such key people as Jeffery Amherst, a British general who led the siege of Louisbourg and the capture of Montreal; William Johnson, a British official who served as commissioner of Indian affairs in the American colonies during the war; Louis-Joseph, marquis de Montcalm-Gozon de Saint-Véran, a French general who handed the British several defeats before he was killed during the Battle of Quebec; Pontiac, an Ottawa chief who led a postwar Indian uprising against the British; and George Washington, an American soldier who went on to lead colonial forces in the American Revolution and serve as the first president of the United States. Each profile features a portrait and an individual "For More Information" section.

Informative sidebars can be found throughout the Almanac and Biographies sections as well. These sidebars contain brief biographies; excerpts from memoirs, speeches, and important documents; and interesting facts about the issues and events discussed in the main body of the text. In addition, approximately sixty paintings, portraits, drawings, and maps illustrate the work.

French and Indian War also includes a timeline of important events, "Words to Know" and "People to Know" sections that combine those terms from individual chapters, and a list of "Research and Activity Ideas" with suggestions for study questions, group projects, and oral and dramatic presentations. *French and Indian War* concludes with a bibliography of sources for further reading and a comprehensive index.

Acknowledgments

Thanks go to copyeditor Rebecca Valentine, proofreader Amy Marcaccio Keyzer, and typesetter Marco Di Vita of the Graphix Group for their fine work.

Comments and suggestions

We welcome your comments on *French and Indian War* and suggestions for other topics in history to consider. Please write: Editors, *French and Indian War*, U•X•L, 27500 Drake Road, Farmington Hills, MI 48331-3535; call toll-free 800-347-4253; fax to 248-699-8097; or send e-mail via www.gale.com.

Words to Know

A

Acadians: French-speaking Catholic residents of Nova Scotia who were deported when the British captured the region in 1755.

Albany Congress: A July 1754 meeting at which American colonial leaders discussed ways for improving relations between the colonies and the Iroquois Confederacy, as well as for presenting a unified defense against the French.

C

Colony: A permanent settlement in a new land formed by citizens who maintain ties to their mother country; both Great Britain and France established colonies in North America.

E

Embargo: A government order that prohibits all commercial ship traffic from entering or leaving a harbor; John

Campbell, fourth earl of Loudoun, placed an embargo on the entire Atlantic coast of America in 1756 in an attempt to stop illegal trading with the French.

F

Forks of the Ohio: French and British forces competed to build a fort on this strategic location, where the Monongahela and Allegheny Rivers join to form the Ohio River (site of modern-day Pittsburgh, Pennsylvania).

I

Iroquois Confederacy (Six Nations of the Iroquois): A powerful alliance of six Indian nations (the Cayuga, Mohawk, Oneida, Onondaga, Seneca, and Tuscarora) from the Iroquois language family.

Irregulars: Soldiers who were not part of the formal British Army, including troops and militia recruited in the American colonies; irregulars tended to have less military training and poorer equipment than British regulars.

O

Ohio Country: A vast wilderness that stretched from the Great Lakes in the north to the Ohio River in the South, and from the Allegheny Mountains in the east to the Mississippi River in the west; the French and British fought for control of this region, which lay between the French and British colonies in North America.

Q

Quakers: Members of the Society of Friends religious group, which originated in England in the seventeenth century and was brought to America by William Penn, founder of Pennsylvania Colony; among the Quakers' main principles was pacifism (a strong opposition to war and violence).

R

Regulars: Professional soldiers of the British Army; they tended to be highly trained and well equipped compared to irregulars from the American colonies.

S

Siege: A military strategy that involves surrounding a target, cutting it off from outside help and supplies, and using artillery to break down its defenses.

Stamp Act: A law passed by British parliament in 1765 that placed a tax on all paper used for legal or business purposes in the American colonies; it met with violent opposition in the colonies and was later repealed.

T

Treaty of Paris: The 1763 agreement between Great Britain and France that ended the French and Indian War (known in Europe as the Seven Years' War); it gave Great Britain control over all the French territory in North America east of the Mississippi River, as well as several French colonies in India, Africa, and the West Indies.

People to Know

A

James Abercromby (1706–1781): British general who served as commander-in-chief of British forces in North America in 1758 and suffered a terrible defeat in the Battle of Ticonderoga.

Jeffery Amherst (1717–1797): British military leader who became commander-in-chief of British forces in North America in 1758 and led the siege of Louisbourg and capture of Montreal.

B

Louis-Antoine de Bougainville (1729–1811): French military leader who served in the defense of Ticonderoga and Quebec; later became the first Frenchman to sail around the world; made several important contributions to science and geography.

Edward Braddock (1695–1755): British military leader who served as commander-in-chief of British forces in

North America in 1755 and was killed in a disastrous early battle on the Monongahela River.

John Bradstreet (c. 1711–1774): British military leader who captured Fort Frontenac and ended French control of Lake Ontario.

John Stuart, third earl of Bute (1713–1792): British political leader who forced William Pitt to resign; served as prime minister of Great Britain, 1761–63.

C

Claude-Pierre Pecaudy, seigneur de Contrecoeur (1706–1775): French military leader who captured the partially finished British fort at the Forks of the Ohio and established Fort Duquesne on the site.

D

Baron Ludwig August (also known as Jean-Armand) Dieskau (1701–1767): French military leader who lost the Battle of Lake George and was wounded and captured by the British.

Robert Dinwiddie (1693–1770): Governor of Virginia Colony who held land claims in the Ohio Country and pressured the British government to take control of the region.

Ange Duquesne de Menneville, marquis de Duquesne (1700–1778): French military leader who became governor-general of New France in 1752 and ordered the construction of a chain of forts across the Ohio Country.

F

John Forbes (1710–1759): British military leader who captured Fort Duquesne in 1758 and established Fort Pitt on the site.

Benjamin Franklin (1706–1790): Wealthy and influential Philadelphia printer who unsuccessfully put forth a plan to unite the British colonies at the Albany Congress; later played important roles in the American Revolution and the drafting of the Constitution.

Louis de Buade, comte de Frontenac (1620–1698): French political leader who served as governor of New France from 1672 to 1682, and again from 1696 to 1698; promoted exploration of Canada, established new forts, and sent Indian allies on raids against British settlements during King William's War.

G

King George III (1738–1820): King of England, 1760–1820; after claiming the throne near the end of the French and Indian War, his policies created resistance in the American colonies that led to the American Revolution.

H

Patrick Henry (1736–1799): American political leader who first gained attention for his opposition to the Stamp Act as a member of the Virginia Assembly; later served in the Continental Congress and as governor of Virginia.

J

William Johnson (1715–1774): British general who served as chief of Indian affairs and won the Battle of Lake George.

Joseph Coulon de Villiers de Jumonville (1718–1754): French military leader who carried a message to Lieutenant Colonel George Washington, was attacked by Washington's forces, and was murdered by Seneca tribe civil chief Tanaghrisson.

L

Jacques Legardeur de Saint-Pierre: French military leader who met with George Washington at Fort Le Boeuf during Washington's 1753 diplomatic mission.

John Campbell, fourth earl of Loudoun: British general who served as commander-in-chief of British forces in North America, 1756–58.

M

Louis-Joseph, marquis de Montcalm-Gozon de Saint-Véran (1712–1759): French general who served as commander-in-chief of French forces in North America, 1756–59; led the capture of Forts Oswego and William Henry and died during the battle for Quebec.

James Murray (c. 1721–1794): British general who served under James Wolfe during the Battle of Quebec and went on to serve as the first British governor of Canada, 1764–68.

P

William Pitt (1708–1788): British political leader who took control of the North American war effort in 1757; his policies gained the support of the American colonists.

Pontiac (c. 1720–1769): Ottawa chief who united Great Lakes Indian tribes in opposition to British rule; led a large-scale Indian rebellion that resulted in the capture of several British forts before surrendering in 1765.

S

William Shirley (1694–1771): Governor of Massachusetts who served as commander-in-chief of British forces in North America following the death of Edward Braddock.

T

Tanaghrisson (?–1754): Seneca civil chief who murdered a French diplomat during George Washington's 1754 attack on French forces that started the French and Indian War.

V

Pierre François de Rigaud, marquis de Vaudreuil (1698–1765): Governor of New France from 1755 until the fall of Canada to the British in 1760.

W

George Washington (1732–1799): American military and political leader who took part in the early battles of the French and Indian War and went on to lead the American Revolution and serve as the first president of the United States.

James Wolfe (1727–1759): British military leader who captured Louisbourg and was killed during the successful battle for Quebec.

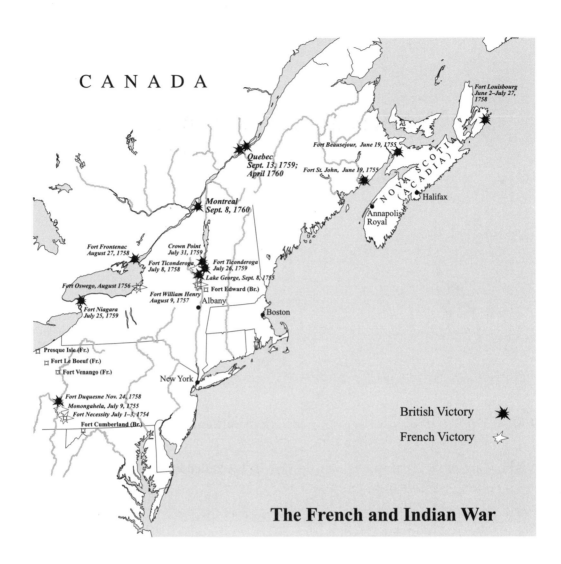

C A N A D A

Fort Louisbourg
June 2–July 27,
1758

Fort Beausejour, June 19, 1755

Fort St. John, June 19, 1755

Quebec
Sept. 13, 1759;
April 1760

NOVA SCOTIA (ACADIA)

Halifax

Annapolis
Royal

Montreal
Sept. 8, 1760

Fort Frontenac
August 27, 1758

Crown Point
July 31, 1759

Fort Ticonderoga
July 26, 1759

Fort Ticonderoga
July 8, 1758

Lake George, Sept. 8, 1755

Fort Oswego, August 1756

Fort William Henry
August 9, 1757

Fort Edward (Br.)

Albany

Fort Niagara
July 25, 1759

Boston

Presque Isle (Fr.)

Fort Le Boeuf (Fr.)

Fort Venango (Fr.)

New York

Fort Duquesne Nov. 24, 1758
Monongahela, July 9, 1755
Fort Necessity July 1–3, 1754

Fort Cumberland (Br.)

British Victory

French Victory

The French and Indian War

French and Indian War Timeline

1607 The British form the first permanent settlement in North America in Jamestown, Virginia.

1608 Samuel de Champlain explores the St. Lawrence River and founds Quebec for France.

1689 King William's War (known in Europe as the War of the League of Augsburg) begins.

1695 British general Edward Braddock is born in England.

1697 King William's War ends.

1701 Queen Anne's War (known in Europe as the War of the Spanish Succession) begins.

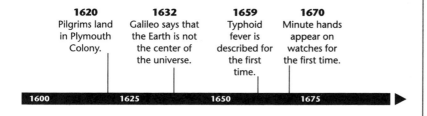

1620	**1632**	**1659**	**1670**
Pilgrims land in Plymouth Colony.	Galileo says that the Earth is not the center of the universe.	Typhoid fever is described for the first time.	Minute hands appear on watches for the first time.

1600　　　　　1625　　　　　1650　　　　　1675

1708	British war minister William Pitt is born in England.
1712	French general Louis-Joseph, marquis de Montcalm-Gozon de Saint-Véran, is born in France.
1713	Queen Anne's War ends.
1715	British general and colonial administrator William Johnson is born in Ireland.
1717	British general Jeffery Amherst is born in England.
1720	The French begin constructing a huge fortress in Louisbourg on Cape Breton Island.
1720	Ottawa chief Pontiac is born in the Great Lakes region of North America.
1727	British general James Wolfe is born in England.
1732	American military and political leader George Washington is born in Virginia.
1744	King George's War (known in Europe as the War of the Austrian Succession) begins.
1744	The Iroquois Confederacy signs the Treaty of Lancaster, giving up land claims in Pennsylvania, Virginia, and Maryland.
1745	American colonists capture Louisbourg from the French.
1748	King George's War ends and Louisbourg is returned to France.
1752	Ange Duquesne de Menneville, marquis de Duquesne, becomes governor-general of New France and builds forts in the Ohio Country.

1704
America's first regular newspaper begins publication.

1714
Daniel Fahrenheit builds a mercury thermometer.

1725
Antonio Vivaldi composes *The Four Seasons.*

1732
Benjamin Franklin revolutionizes the colonial postal service.

1700	1715	1730	1745

1753   Colonial messenger and future military and political leader George Washington carries a message from British leaders asking the French to leave the Ohio Country.

1754   The French and Indian War begins in North America.

1754   In May, Indians accompanying Lieutenant Colonel George Washington murder French officer Joseph Coulon de Villiers de Jumonville.

1754   In July, American military leader George Washington is defeated by French forces in the Battle of Fort Necessity.

1755   British general Edward Braddock becomes commander-in-chief of the British forces in North America.

1755   William Johnson becomes British commissioner of Indian affairs in the northern colonies.

1755   In June, British forces capture Fort Beauséjour and take control of Nova Scotia.

1755   In July, British general Edward Braddock's army is defeated by French and Indian forces in the Battle of the Wilderness; Braddock dies of his wounds from the battle.

1755   In September, the British deport from Nova Scotia the French-speaking Catholics known as Acadians.

1755   In September, British general and colonial administrator William Johnson defeats French forces in the Battle of Lake George.

1756   Great Britain and France formally declare war (the conflict becomes known in Europe as the Seven Years' War).

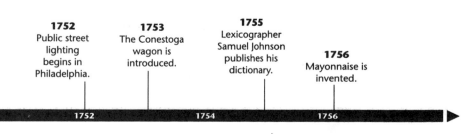

1752
Public street lighting begins in Philadelphia.

1753
The Conestoga wagon is introduced.

1755
Lexicographer Samuel Johnson publishes his dictionary.

1756
Mayonnaise is invented.

1750   1752   1754   1756

1756 John Campbell, fourth earl of Loudoun, becomes commander-in-chief of British forces in North America.

1756 French general Louis-Joseph, marquis de Montcalm-Gozon de Saint-Véran, arrives to command French forces in North America.

1756 In August, the French capture Fort Oswego on Lake Ontario from the British.

1757 British secretary of state William Pitt takes over the British war effort.

1757 In August, the French capture Fort William Henry on Lake George, and their Indian allies massacre British prisoners.

1758 British general James Abercromby becomes commander-in-chief of British forces in North America.

1758 In July, British general Jeffery Amherst captures Louisbourg from the French.

1758 In July, British general James Abercromby loses the Battle of Ticonderoga.

1758 In August, British forces under Lieutenant Colonel John Bradstreet capture Fort Frontenac on Lake Ontario.

1758 In November, British forces under Major General John Forbes capture Fort Duquesne at the Forks of the Ohio River.

1758 In November, British general Jeffery Amherst becomes commander-in-chief of British forces in North America.

1759 In July, British general and colonial administrator William Johnson captures Fort Niagara.

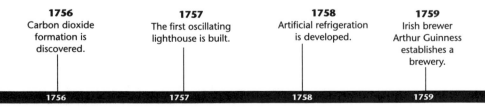

1756
Carbon dioxide formation is discovered.

1757
The first oscillating lighthouse is built.

1758
Artificial refrigeration is developed.

1759
Irish brewer Arthur Guinness establishes a brewery.

1756   1757   1758   1759

1759   In July, British general Jeffery Amherst captures Ticonderoga and Fort St. Frédéric on Lake Champlain.

1759   In September, British general James Wolfe defeats French general Louis-Joseph, marquis de Montcalm-Gozon de Saint-Véran, in the Battle of Quebec; both are killed in the battle.

1760   The French surrender Montreal and all other territory in North America to the British.

1760   The Cherokee War strikes the southern American colonies.

1760   King George II dies and is succeeded on the throne by King George III.

1761   British war minister William Pitt resigns from the British government.

1762   Spain joins the Seven Years' War on the side of the French.

1763   The Treaty of Paris ends the war.

1763   Pontiac leads an Indian rebellion that succeeds in capturing several British forts.

1763   The British government passes the Proclamation Act to prevent settlers from moving into the Ohio Country.

1764   The British government passes new taxes on the colonies: the American Duties Act (Sugar Act) and the Currency Act.

1765   The British government passes the Stamp Act, which meets with violent opposition in the American colonies.

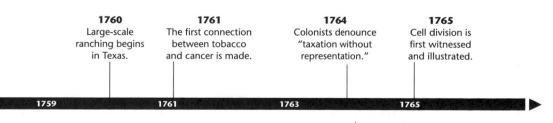

1760
Large-scale ranching begins in Texas.

1761
The first connection between tobacco and cancer is made.

1764
Colonists denounce "taxation without representation."

1765
Cell division is first witnessed and illustrated.

1759   1761   1763   1765

1765 American wilderness fighter Robert Rogers publishes *Reminiscences of the French War,* a famous account of his days as a ranger.

1766 French officer Louis-Antoine de Bougainville sails around the world.

1769 Ottawa chief Pontiac is killed in Illinois.

1774 British general and colonial administrator William Johnson dies in New York.

1775 The American Revolution begins.

1775 The Continental Congress selects American military and political leader George Washington to command the colonial army.

1778 British war minister William Pitt dies in London.

1787 The U.S. Constitution is written.

1789 American military leader George Washington becomes the first president of the United States.

1797 British general Jeffery Amherst dies in England.

1799 Former U.S. president and military leader George Washington dies in Virginia.

1826 James Fenimore Cooper publishes *Last of the Mohicans,* a famous novel set during the French and Indian War.

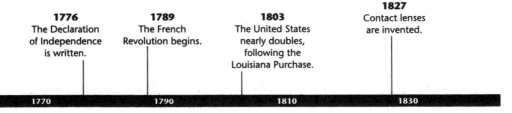

1776
The Declaration of Independence is written.

1789
The French Revolution begins.

1803
The United States nearly doubles, following the Louisiana Purchase.

1827
Contact lenses are invented.

1770   1790   1810   1830

Research and Activity Ideas

The following research and activity ideas are intended to offer suggestions for complementing social studies and history curricula, to trigger additional ideas for enhancing learning, and to provide cross-disciplinary projects for library and classroom use.

- The French and Indian War has been called the first true world war. In fact, some historians claim that the French and Indian War was more significant in the eyes of the world than the American Revolution. Make a list of reasons that may have caused historians to reach this conclusion. How would North America and the world be different today if the French had won the war?

- Look at a map of the French and British colonies in North America before the start of the French and Indian War. Why would the two sides fight for control of the Ohio Country? What made the Forks of the Ohio River (where the French built Fort Duquesne and the British later built Fort Pitt) such an important target for both sides? Divide the class into three groups. One group will defend France's claim on the Ohio Country, one group will explain Great Britain's stake in the region, and the third group will argue that the territory rightfully belonged to the Indians (Native Americans).

- The Indian tribes that had lived in the Ohio Country for many generations found themselves caught in the middle of the dispute between the British and French for control of the region. How did the Indians decide which side to support? Research the life of a Native American leader who lived during the French and Indian War. Some examples include Captain Jacobs, Hendrick, Pontiac, Shingas, Scarouady, and Tanaghrisson. Taking the perspective of the Indian chief you have chosen, make an oral presentation in which you try to convince the class (your tribe) to support either the French or the British.

- British forces under General Edward Braddock suffered a terrible defeat in the first major battle of the French and Indian War. Research the weapons and fighting style of the British Army and compare them to those of the French and Native Americans. Which style of warfare was better suited to conditions in North America? Write a report outlining the mistakes Braddock made and the effects of the British defeat.

- When British forces captured Fort Beauséjour and took control of Nova Scotia in 1755, they decided to deport the French-speaking Catholic residents of the region, who were known as Acadians. Over six thousand Acadians were packed onto ships and transported to the American colonies, where they had trouble fitting in and suffered many hardships. Imagine that you are an Acadian and have been forced to leave your home and settle in an unfamiliar land. Write an account of your imaginary experiences as an outsider in colonial America. This account could take the form of a diary, a letter to a family member who remained in Nova Scotia, or a letter of protest to British authorities.

- Divide the class into several groups. Have each group prepare an oral presentation about a major battle of the French and Indian War, with group members playing the roles of generals, soldiers, and political leaders on each side. The presentation should conclude with a report on how classmates can visit the site of the battle today.

- Using historical maps and drawings, create a three-dimensional model of Quebec as it appeared in 1759. Be sure to include the cliffs overlooking the St. Lawrence River, the walled city with its cannons, and the Plains of Abraham. How did Quebec's natural defenses influence the battle? Were the British lucky to have captured the city?

- The French commander Louis-Joseph, marquis de Montcalm-Gozon de Saint-Véran, was a brilliant general who handed the British a series of defeats in the early years of the French and Indian War. Yet Montcalm and the French could not hold their advantage and ended up losing the Battle of Quebec and control of North America. Make a list of the factors that favored the French and the British at the beginning of the war. How had these factors changed by the time Montcalm faced the British in the Battle of Quebec? Make another list of the factors that made Montcalm's job difficult and ultimately led to his defeat.

- Select a state that was one of the thirteen original American colonies. Create a timeline of important events in that state during colonial times, including its role during the French and Indian War.

- Read James Fenimore Cooper's novel *Last of the Mohicans*, which is set during the French and Indian War. Pick out the author's references to actual wartime events. How does Cooper use historical references to advance the central theme of his story?

- The French and Indian War changed the relationship between Great Britain and its American colonies. Some historians claim that these changes led directly to the American Revolution. Make a list of the changes that resulted from the war. Rank these factors in order of importance as causes of the American Revolution. If the French and British had settled their differences peacefully instead of fighting for control of North America, do you think the War of Independence still would have happened ten years later?

- The French and Indian War shaped the lives of its participants and influenced future events in many ways. Think about how George Washington's life would have been different had he not fought in the war. Tell the class about a personal experience that has had a significant impact on the future direction of your life.

- Mark the locations of major forts and battles of the French and Indian War on a modern-day map of eastern North America. What cities have grown up on these spots? Are the locations that were important during the war still important today? Do you recognize any place names from the region's history?

Almanac

Events Leading to the French and Indian War

1

The French and Indian War is part of an often-forgotten period in American history. It took place from 1754 to 1763—between the time the first European settlers arrived in North America and the time when some of their descendants fought for independence in the American Revolution (1775–83). The French and Indian War (known in Europe as the Seven Years' War) was the fourth in a series of wars between Great Britain and France, fought to determine which European country would emerge as the world's dominant power. Unlike the first three wars, though, this one started in the North American colonies held by British and French settlers. On one side of the fight were British soldiers, settlers from the thirteen American colonies, and several Indian (Native American) tribes. On the other side were French soldiers, settlers from the colony of New France, and their Indian allies.

The French and Indian War played an important role in shaping both American and world history. In fact, some historians claim that the conflict was more significant than the American Revolution in the eyes of the world. The conflict involved three continents and claimed hundreds of thousands of lives; it

Words to Know

Colony: A permanent settlement in a new land formed by citizens who maintain ties to their mother country; both Great Britain and France established colonies in North America.

Iroquois Confederacy (Six Nations of the Iroquois): A powerful alliance of six Indian nations (the Cayuga, Mohawk, Oneida, Onondaga, Seneca, and Tuscarora) from the Iroquois language family.

Ohio Country: A vast wilderness that stretched from the Great Lakes in the north to the Ohio River in the south, and from the Allegheny Mountains in the east to the Mississippi River in the west; the French and British fought for control of this region, which lay between the French and British colonies in North America.

could legitimately be considered the first world war. In addition, the French and Indian War was the first eighteenth-century conflict that ended in a dramatic victory for one side. By winning the war, Great Britain gained control over all of North America east of the Mississippi River and expanded the British empire around the world. But the conflict also created serious problems between the British government and the American colonies. These differences ultimately led to the creation of the United States of America.

Europeans settle in North America

The story of the French and Indian War begins with the arrival of European settlers in the New World. The British formed their first permanent settlement in North America in Jamestown, Virginia, in 1607. The French founded the capital of New France in Quebec (a present-day province of Canada) a year later. For many years, the vast wilderness that stretched between these colonies ensured that the French and British settlers would have little contact with each other.

The French government viewed its colony in North America as a source of furs and other valuable trade goods, rather than as a place to be settled. The people who came to New France in its early years were mostly explorers and traders, although several busy towns eventually developed. On the other hand, the British government viewed its North American territory as a land that would provide new homes for poor and dissatisfied British citizens. British leaders actively promoted settlement in America and allowed the colonists to form their own governments, with governors approved by the king of England.

Over time, it became clear that the North American colonies could produce tremendous wealth for the nations of Europe through farming, logging, mining, fur trapping, and other activities. With this in mind, several European countries fought for control over sections of North America, including Spain and Denmark. By the early 1700s, however, Great Britain and France held most of the territory east of the Mississippi River. The British colonies consisted of scattered towns and villages stretching along the Atlantic Coast, from present-day Maine to Georgia. Meanwhile, the French controlled eastern Canada and parts of the Great Lakes region and the Mississippi River basin.

People to Know

Louis de Buade, comte de Frontenac (1620–1698): French political leader who served as governor of New France from 1672 to 1682, and again from 1696 to 1698; promoted exploration of Canada, established new forts, and sent Indian allies on raids against British settlements during King William's War.

Indians occupy middle ground between France and England

By the time the first European settlers arrived, North America was already home to millions of Indians. These peoples had developed a wide range of cultures over thousands of years. Some tribes lived in large, permanent settlements of several thousand residents, while others spent most of their time traveling in search of food and game. Some of the tribes maintained peaceful relations with neighboring peoples, while other tribes were constantly at war with one another.

For the most part, the French people who came to North America got along well with the Indians. They traded fairly with the tribes, learned their ways, and did not push them off of their traditional lands. French priests even converted many Great Lakes tribes to the Catholic religion. But the more numerous British settlers needed more land for their farming operations. As a result, they pushed into areas that were previously inhabited only by Indians, who came to be viewed as obstacles to further settlement.

The British settlers maintained good relations only with the tribes of the Iroquois Confederacy, an alliance of six

Pilgrims, some of the earliest English colonists, arrive at Plymouth Rock in Massachusetts in 1620.
Reproduced by permission of Getty Images.

Indian nations from the Iroquois language family (Cayuga, Mohawk, Oneida, Onondaga, Seneca, and Tuscarora) centered in northern New York. The Iroquois had held a grudge against the French since the early 1600s when, during one of the first European expeditions into North America, French explorer Samuel de Champlain (c. 1567–1635) had shot several Iroquois warriors with the first firearm they had ever seen.

As the French and British settlements grew, the Indians were pushed into the middle ground between the European colonies. The Iroquois Confederacy formed an alliance with the British in order to control trade and prevent the French from expanding their territory. Meanwhile, the French formed a system of alliances with Algonquian-speaking tribes of the Great Lakes region, including the Pequot, Illinois, Kickapoo, Menomini, Miami, Chippewa, Ottawa, and Potawatomi. Many of the Algonquian peoples were longtime enemies of the Iroquois.

Two members of the Iroquois tribe address other Indian tribes. *Illustration by John Kahionhes Fadden. Reproduced by permission of John Kahionhes Fadden.*

Three early wars

Throughout the late 1600s and early 1700s, Great Britain and France struggled to become the most dominant power in Europe. The two countries entered into three wars during these years. All of these wars were fought primarily in Europe. But even though an ocean separated Europe from North America, these wars had a significant influence on the lives of many French and British settlers in the "New World." King William's War (known in Europe as the War of the League of Augsburg) took place between 1689 and 1697. In North America, French and British forces fought to decide who would control the major rivers that ran through the Appalachian Mountains. (Rivers acted as roads in those days because it was so difficult to carry goods through woods and over mountains.)

The conflict began when the governor of New France, Louis de Buade, comte de Frontenac (1620–1698), ordered his

Louis de Buade, comte de Frontenac. *Courtesy of the Library of Congress.*

Indian allies to conduct violent raids on the British colonies in New England. The Indians killed hundreds of British settlers in a series of raids along the frontier over the next few years. The British responded by launching an attack against New France. They succeeded in capturing Port Royal in Nova Scotia (a present-day province of Canada), but they failed in an attempt to take Quebec. The conflict ended shortly after Frontenac died in 1697. As part of the peace process in Europe, British negotiators returned Nova Scotia to France.

Peace lasted only a few years, though, as Queen Anne's War (known in Europe as the War of the Spanish Succession) began in 1701. This conflict began when the Spanish throne became vacant and both Great Britain and France tried to ensure that one of their allies became the new king of Spain. In North America, the Iroquois Confederacy signed an agreement with France in which they promised to remain neutral in the growing conflict. The governor of New France, Philippe de Rigaud, marquis de Vaudreuil (1643–1725), then sent his Indian allies on raids against British settlements outside of Iroquois control—in Maine, New Hampshire, and Massachusetts. The most famous of these raids took place in Deerfield, Massachusetts, in February 1704, when fifty-six men, women, and children were killed and more than one hundred more were forced to march through the cold into Canada.

The British responded to the raids by launching a major military expedition to conquer Canada in 1711. British ships carried six thousand troops up the Atlantic coast to the mouth of the St. Lawrence River, which provided access to

the inland cities of Quebec and Montreal. But the ships lost their way in a heavy fog, and several of them crashed on the rocks and sank. About one thousand people drowned, forcing the British admiral to call off the expedition.

The war in Europe ended in a British victory in 1713. Great Britain claimed several French territories in Canada, including the Hudson Bay region, Newfoundland, and Nova Scotia. But the peace treaty that ended the war left some boundaries between the colonies unclear. These uncertainties opened the door to future conflicts.

In 1720, the French began building a huge fort in Louisbourg, on Cape Breton Island. Ownership of this large island, located just north of Nova Scotia at the mouth of the St. Lawrence River, remained in dispute at the time. The French wanted to claim the island in order to prevent the British from controlling the St. Lawrence. The new fort had stone walls that were thirty feet high, ten feet thick, and topped with one hundred heavy guns.

General William Pepperell rides triumphantly among his troops after the surrender of Louisbourg in 1745. *Reproduced by permission of Getty Images.*

By the time King George's War (known in Europe as the war of the Austrian Succession) began in 1744, though, only seven hundred French troops were stationed in Louisbourg. The American colonies sent an army of four thousand men under General William Pepperell (1696–1759) to attack Louisbourg in 1745. These forces captured several French cannons that had been abandoned across the harbor from Louisbourg and used them to bombard the fort. The small number of French defenders surrendered the fort a short time later. The American colonists were very proud of their conquest. When the war ended in 1748, however, the terms of the peace treaty returned Cape Breton Island to France.

William Pepperell, American general in charge of the army that attacked Louisbourg in 1745.
Reproduced by permission of Getty Images.

Stage is set for the French and Indian War

As British and French forces fought for control of North America throughout the early eighteenth century, the Iroquois Confederacy remained on the sidelines. Yet the Iroquois played an important role in maintaining the balance of power in North America. Indian nations that were loyal to the confederacy controlled the vast territory between the French and British colonies, known as the Ohio Country. The Iroquois traded with both sides, accepted their gifts, and played the European powers against each other for their own benefit.

But the Iroquois Confederacy gradually began losing its influence over other Indian nations as well as the British and French. In 1742, the Iroquois accepted a controversial land deal known as the Walking Purchase of 1737. In this deal, the Penn family (founders of Pennsylvania Colony) stole 670,000 acres in eastern Pennsylvania from the Delaware Indian tribe. The Delawares were forced to relocate to the Ohio Country, and they held a grudge against the confederacy from that time forward.

The Iroquois lost even more of their power in 1744, when they signed the Treaty of Lancaster. Under this agreement, the British gave the Iroquois a huge number of gifts and acknowledged that the confederacy had the authority to speak for its member tribes throughout the Ohio Country. In exchange, the Iroquois agreed to give up all remaining Indian land claims in the colonies of Pennsylvania, Virginia, and Maryland. In reality, however, the Treaty of Lancaster was much more costly for the Iroquois Confederacy. The Indians who negotiated the treaty thought they were only giving the British a small parcel of land in the Shenandoah Valley. But the original charters (written documents that define the boundaries of property and grant rights to landowners) for these colonies said that their borders extended all the way to the Pacific Ocean. Without realizing it, the Iroquois had given up formal control over the Ohio Country.

Once the Treaty of Lancaster was signed, governors of the American colonies immediately began granting land rights in the Ohio Country to their citizens. British traders and settlers rushed to claim the territory. They set up huge trading posts, including one on the site of the modern-day city of Cleveland, and began trading with northern Indian tribes that were supposed to be French allies. French leaders grew alarmed at this turn of events. They were upset about facing new competition in trade with the Indians, and they worried that the availability of British goods would lure away their Indian allies. They were also angry that the British were trying to control the Ohio Country, which they felt belonged to France. In the meantime, the Indians wanted to prevent either European power from claiming the Ohio Country, where they had lived for many generations. This tense situation soon erupted into war.

1753: Washington's Diplomatic Mission

2

In the eighteenth century, France and Great Britain were the world's superpowers. Both nations had expanded the reach of their empires by establishing colonies (permanent settlements of citizens that maintain ties to their home country) in North America and other regions of the world. Great Britain's colonies in North America stretched along the east coast of what later became the United States, from present-day Maine to Georgia. France's territory in North America, known as New France, included parts of modern Canada along the St. Lawrence River, as well as the Great Lakes region and the Mississippi River from Illinois all the way to Louisiana. France and Great Britain had been fighting over their colonial possessions—in North America and around the world—for many years.

In between the French and British territories in North America lay a vast wilderness known as the Ohio Country. This region stretched from the Great Lakes in the north to the Ohio River in the south, and from the Allegheny Mountains in the east to the Mississippi River in the west. It included parts of present-day Pennsylvania, Ohio, West Virginia, Kentucky, Indiana, and Illinois. Both France and Great Britain hoped to extend their colonies into the Ohio Country, which offered settlers access to fertile farmland and the valuable fur trade. But neither European power was able to take control of the Ohio Country because this middle ground was held by the Iroquois Confederacy (also known as the Six Nations of the Iroquois). The confederacy was a powerful alliance of six Indian (Native American) nations from the Iroquois language family—the Cayuga, Mohawk, Oneida, Onondaga, Seneca, and Tuscarora.

The Six Nations' hold on the Ohio Country began to break down during the 1740s. As more British and French traders moved into the region, they were able to form relationships with many Indian tribes. Tribes that were once loyal to the Iroquois Confederacy were gradually lured away by the availability of French and British goods. This situation reduced the influence of the Iroquois Confederacy and shook up the balance of power in the Ohio Country. Both France and Great Britain were eager to take advantage of the situation in order to increase the size of their territorial holdings.

France wanted to control the Ohio Country because it provided an important connection between the French colonies in Canada and those in Illinois and along the Mississippi River. French leaders also knew that claiming the region would create a barrier to keep the British colonies from expanding westward beyond the Allegheny Mountains. But Great Britain also recognized the strategic value of the Ohio Country. British leaders wanted to control the region so they could continue expanding their colonies westward and gain access to the land's rich natural resources. They also knew that claiming the area would divide the French territories and make them easier to conquer.

Words to Know

Iroquois Confederacy (Six Nations of the Iroquois): A powerful alliance of six Indian nations (the Cayuga, Mohawk, Oneida, Onondaga, Seneca, and Tuscarora) from the Iroquois language family.

Ohio Country: A vast wilderness that stretched from the Great Lakes in the north to the Ohio River in the South, and from the Allegheny Mountains in the east to the Mississippi River in the west; the French and British fought for control of this region, which lay between the French and British colonies in North America.

People to Know

Robert Dinwiddie (1693–1770): Lieutenant governor of Virginia Colony who held land claims in the Ohio Country and pressured the British government to take control of the region. Two other men held the ceremonial title of governor, but never set foot in Virginia; Dinwiddie, therefore, was always considered the head of the colony and usually referred to as the governor.

Ange Duquesne de Menneville, marquis de Duquesne (1700–1778): French military leader who became governor-general of New France in 1752 and ordered the construction of a chain of forts across the Ohio Country.

Jacques Legardeur de Saint-Pierre (1701–1755): French military leader who met with George Washington at Fort Le Boeuf during Washington's 1753 diplomatic mission.

George Washington (1732–1799): American military and political leader who took part in the early battles of the French and Indian War and went on to lead the American Revolution and serve as the first president of the United States.

Competing claims on the land

In 1752, Ange Duquesne de Menneville, marquis de Duquesne (1700–1778) became governor-general of New France. A no-nonsense fellow who had served in the French Navy, Duquesne was determined to take control of the Ohio Country. He carried orders from the French government that said he should "make every effort to drive the English from our lands." To carry out this mission, he started building a chain of forts from Lake Erie southward to the Ohio River. Once they were completed, these four forts—Presque Isle on Lake Erie, Le Boeuf on French Creek, Machault at the settlement of Venango in modern-day Pennsylvania, and Duquesne at the junction of the Monongahela and Allegheny Rivers (a spot known as the Forks of the Ohio)—would effectively prevent British traders and settlers from going west.

At the same time, wealthy and influential men from the Virginia and Pennsylvania colonies convinced King George II (1683–1760) of England to grant them title to land in the Ohio Country. One group of land speculators (people who buy and sell land with the hope of making a profit) formed an association called the Ohio Company. The members of this group included Lawrence Washington (1718–1752), the older half-brother of **George Washington** (1732–1799; see entry), and Lieutenant Governor Robert Dinwiddie (1693–1770; see box) of Virginia Colony. The Ohio Company received a grant of five hundred thousand acres along the Ohio River from the British government. When Lawrence Washington died of tu-

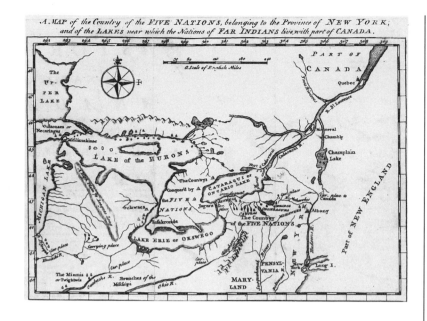

A MAP of the Country of the FIVE NATIONS, belonging to the Province of NEW YORK; and of the LAKES near which the Nations of FAR INDIANS live, with part of CANADA.

A 1723 map shows the Five Nations, the Great Lakes, and eastern territory. The Five Nations became Six Nations when the Tuscarora tribe left its land in North Carolina and moved north. *Reproduced by permission of Getty Images.*

berculosis (a disease that affects the lungs) in 1752, George inherited some of his land claims.

The members of the Ohio Company knew that their claim to this land would be worthless if France controlled the Ohio Country. In order to protect their interests, they wanted to prevent the French from building their forts. They convinced the British government, which was already concerned about France gaining power in North America, that military action might be needed. In 1753, British authorities gave Lieutenant Governor Dinwiddie permission to build forts in the Ohio Country and to remove the French by force if necessary. But he was only allowed to use force in response to hostile acts by the French.

Washington brings a message to the French

Dinwiddie decided to send a message to French leaders in the Ohio Country. The message would inform the French that the king of England had claimed the region. It would also demand that the French stop building forts and leave the Ohio Country. "The lands upon the River Ohio, in the western parts of the colony of Virginia, are so notoriously

Robert Dinwiddie, Lieutenant Governor of Virginia

Robert Dinwiddie was a wealthy Scottish merchant who became a leading voice in support of expanding the British Empire deep into the North American wilderness. Dinwiddie was born in 1693 in Scotland, where his father had built a successful business career. Upon reaching adulthood, Dinwiddie followed in his father's footsteps as a prosperous merchant. In 1721, however, he was appointed to serve as administrator of Bermuda, which was a British territory at the time.

After spending sixteen years in Bermuda, Dinwiddie was promoted to the position of surveyor general in the American colonies. As a leading authority over Pennsylvania and several southern colonies, he gained a reputation for firm decision-making and devotion to the British Crown. On July 4, 1751, Dinwiddie was named lieutenant governor of Virginia, England's largest colony in North America. (He was always considered the head of the colony since the two men who held the ceremonial title of governor never set foot in Virginia.) Dinwiddie thus became one of the most powerful figures in all of the colonies.

Dinwiddie strongly supported British efforts to expand their holdings in North America, and he viewed the French and their Indian allies as serious obstacles to that goal. In addition, he saw an opportunity to increase his wealth by harvesting the abundant natural resources of the western forests. As a result, he urged the colonies to create and supply their own military force and called for the use of regular British troops in America. In 1753, the British government gave Dinwiddie permission to establish forts in the Ohio River Valley and other regions.

Eager to claim western lands, Dinwiddie sent a young colonist named George Washington on a mission to a French outpost located deep in the disputed Ohio Country. Washington told the

[widely] known to be the property of the Crown of Great Britain that it is a matter of equal concern and surprise to me, to hear that a body of French forces are erecting [building] fortresses and making settlements upon that river, within his Majesty's dominions [area of ownership or authority]," Dinwiddie wrote in his message to the French. "It becomes my duty to require your peaceable departure."

Since there were no telephones or telegraphs in those days, Dinwiddie had to send a messenger into the wilderness. He selected a young man named George Wash-

Robert Dinwiddie. *Courtesy of the Library of Congress.*

French to stop building forts in the region and to make way for English settlement. The French scoffed at Washington's message, which angered Dinwiddie. The following year, he promoted Washington to lieutenant colonel in the Virginia militia and sent him back into the wilderness with two hundred soldiers. According to Dinwiddie's orders, Washington was to use his army to defend Fort Prince George (modern-day Pittsburgh, Pennsylvania) from enemy attack. But the expedition encountered a wide range of troubles, including the murder of a captured French officer by **Tanaghrisson** (?–1754; see box in Chapter 3), an Indian chieftain who had been traveling with Washington. This murder is often cited as the event that triggered the French and Indian War (known in Europe as the Seven Years' War).

As the French and Indian War roared to life, Dinwiddie struggled to take care of all his duties as a colonial administrator. He became so concerned about the war and supervising Virginia's affairs that his health suffered. In 1758, he was relieved of office at his own request, and he and his family returned to England. Dinwiddie died in London on July 27, 1770.

ington. At first glance, Washington seemed like an unlikely person to perform such an important mission. He was only twenty-one years old, had little military or diplomatic experience, and could not speak French. But Washington was an ambitious young man, eager to take on the dangerous task. He was also a capable horseman who had developed strong outdoor skills by working as a surveyor (a person who measures and marks the boundaries of tracts of land). Finally, Washington shared the governor's interest in securing the Ohio Company's land claims because he had inherited some of his brother's shares.

George Washington, who acted as an important messenger for Virginia lieutenant governor Robert Dinwiddie. *Reproduced by permission of Getty Images.*

In late October 1753, Washington set out on horseback from Williamsburg, Virginia, with a group of six other men to deliver Dinwiddie's message to the French fort at Venango. One member of his group was Jacob Van Braam, a friend of the Washington family who spoke French and could act as a translator. He was also accompanied by Christopher Gist (c. 1706–1759), a frontiersman and Ohio Company agent who served as a guide. Rounding out the group were four other woodsmen who acted as bodyguards and servants.

Washington and his group faced a difficult journey through unfamiliar territory (see box). The late fall weather was cold and rainy, with occasional snow. As they followed the Youghiogheny River to the Monongahela River and then to the Ohio River, it took them more than a week to travel seventy-five miles. Washington gathered information about the land and French activities in the region along the way to Venango. When he reached the Forks, where the Monongahela and Allegheny Rivers join to form the Ohio (the site of modern-day Pittsburgh, Pennsylvania), he noted that it would be an ideal spot for a fort. "The land in the forks I think extremely well situated for a fort, as it has the absolute command of both rivers," he wrote in his journal. "The land at the point is twenty or twenty-five feet above the common surface of the water; and a considerable bottom of flat, well-timbered land all around it, very convenient for building."

During his journey, Washington also discovered that the Indians who lived in the region had little interest in helping the British. Hoping to convince the French that the Indians were his allies, he had invited representatives of several tribes to accompany his men to their meeting with the French. But only a handful of Indians accepted his invitation, including the Seneca leader Tanaghrisson (also known as Half

King). Tanaghrisson was a representative of the Iroquois Confederacy among the tribes of the Ohio Country. His job was to keep these tribes loyal to the confederacy, which also meant keeping them loyal to himself.

When Washington reached Venango, the French soldiers there told him that he needed to meet with their commander, Captain Jacques Legardeur de Saint-Pierre (1701–1755). Legardeur was stationed at Fort Le Boeuf, another sixty miles up French Creek. Leaving their horses at Venango, Washington and his men proceeded to the fort in canoes and on foot. They arrived and delivered their message on December 11.

French politely refuse to leave

Legardeur was not impressed with young Washington and his rough-looking group of men. But the French commander treated them politely and allowed them to stay for several days while he prepared a reply to Dinwiddie's message. Although he agreed to pass the message along to Marquis Duquesne, Legardeur also made it clear that the French had no intention of leaving the Ohio Country. "As to the summons [warning notice] you send me to retire [leave], I do not think myself obliged [bound or required] to obey it," he wrote to Dinwiddie. "Whatever may be your instructions, mine bring me here by my general's order; and I entreat [ask] you, Sir, to be assured that I shall attempt to follow them with all the exactness and determination which can be expected from a good officer."

Washington left Fort Le Boeuf on December 16 with Legardeur's reply. He and his party knew they had to hurry back to Williamsburg to tell Dinwiddie about the French plans. Winter was upon them, and they did not want to be delayed until spring. Washington and his men paddled furiously down French Creek, which had begun to freeze over. When they arrived at Venango, they found that their horses had become too weak to carry riders. So they set off on foot as the temperature dropped and snow began falling. Some of Washington's men got frostbite and had to be left behind in a small hunting shack. Washington pressed on with his guide, Christopher Gist, shedding some of their supplies so that they could travel light.

George Washington (right) and his guide, Christopher Gist, travel on a raft on the Allegheny River on their way to deliver a message to Virginia lieutenant governor Robert Dinwiddie informing him that the French had no intention of leaving the Ohio Country. *Reproduced by permission of Getty Images.*

Washington and Gist made a dangerous journey through the wilderness. In fact, Washington almost lost his life on two different occasions. Once an Indian shot at him at close range and narrowly missed. Later, he fell into the freezing water of the Allegheny River while trying to cross it on a makeshift log raft. Washington saved himself from drowning by throwing an arm across the raft. But Gist was unable to pole the raft to shore by himself, and they ended up drifting onto a small island instead. After spending a cold night there, the two men were thrilled when the morning light showed that the river had frozen over. They walked across and arrived back in Williamsburg on January 16, 1754, eleven weeks after they had set out.

Upon hearing Washington's story, Dinwiddie gave him twenty-four hours to write a detailed report of his journey through the Ohio Country and his meeting with the French. In this report, Washington wrote that Legardeur "told me that the country belonged [to the French]; that no Eng-

Excerpt from George Washington's Journal

George Washington kept a journal during his mission to the Ohio Country in 1753. The following excerpt describes his dangerous winter journey back to Williamsburg, Virginia:

> The horses became less able to travel every day; the cold increased very fast; and the roads were becoming much worse by a deep snow, continually freezing; therefore, as I was uneasy to get back, to make my report of my proceedings to his Honor the Governor [Robert Dinwiddie of Virginia], I determined to prosecute [continue] my journey, the nearest way through the woods, on foot....

> I took my necessary papers, pulled off my clothes, and tied myself up in a watch-coat. Then, with gun in hand, and pack on my back, in which were my papers and provisions, I set out with Mr. [Christopher] Gist [a frontiersman and guide], fitted in the same manner, on Wednesday the 26th [of December, 1753]. The day following ... we fell in with a party of French Indians, who had lain in wait for us. One of them fired at Mr. Gist or me, not fifteen steps off, but fortunately missed. We took this fellow into custody, and kept him until about nine o'clock at night, then let him go, and walked all the remaining part of the night without making any stop, that we might get the start so far, as to be out of the reach of their pursuit the next day, since we were well assured they would follow our track as soon as it was light. The next day we continued traveling until quite dark, and got to the [Allegheny] river about two miles above Shannopins [a small settlement near modern-day Pittsburgh, Pennsylvania]. We ex-pected to have found the river frozen, but it was not, only about fifty yards from each shore. The ice, I suppose, had broken up above, for it was driving in vast quantities.

> There was no way for getting over but on a raft, which we set about [building], with but one poor hatchet, and finished just after sun-setting. This was a whole day's work; we next got it launched, then went on board of it, and set off; but before we were half way over, we were jammed in the ice in such a manner, that we expected every moment our raft to sink, and ourselves to perish. I put out my setting-pole to try to stop the raft, that the ice might pass by, when the rapidity of the stream threw it with so much violence against the pole, that it jerked me out into ten feet water; but I fortunately saved myself by catching hold of one of the raft-logs. Notwithstanding all our efforts, we could not get to either shore, but were obliged, as we were near an island, to quit our raft and make to it.

> The cold was so extremely severe, that Mr. Gist had all his fingers and some of his toes frozen, and the water was shut up so hard, that we had no difficulty in getting off the island on the ice in the morning.

Washington spent two more weeks traveling in cold, wet weather before he finally reached Williamsburg on January 16, 1754, and made his report to Lieutenant Governor Dinwiddie.

Source: Harrison, Maureen, and Steve Gilbert, eds. George Washington in His Own Words. New York: Barnes and Noble Books, 1997.

lishman had a right to trade upon those waters; and that he had orders to make every person prisoner who attempted it on the Ohio, or the waters of it." Dinwiddie sent copies of the report to the Virginia Assembly and to the British government in London.

This famous document made a strong impact on British and colonial leaders. They decided that the French had committed a hostile act by refusing to stop building forts and leave the Ohio Country. They gave Dinwiddie the authority to use force to drive the French out, or at least prevent them from further strengthening their position. The governor ordered an army of two hundred men to be sent to the Forks of the Ohio. This army, led by Washington, would be charged with defending Virginia's land interests against further French advances. Dinwiddie also ordered the construction of a British fort at the Forks—the same strategic spot where Marquis Duquesne planned to build the fourth French fort.

1754: The Fighting Begins

3

The colonial interests of the French and British in North America collided in early 1754 at the Forks of the Ohio River, the strategic spot where the Monongahela and Allegheny Rivers join to form the Ohio River. Robert Dinwiddie (1693–1770; see box in chapter 2), the lieutenant governor of the British colony of Virginia who held land claims in the disputed Ohio Country, sent a group of workers to build a British fort at the Forks in February of that year. (Dinwiddie was always considered the head of the colony since the two men who held the ceremonial title of governor never set foot in Virginia.) Dinwiddie also told **George Washington** (1732–1799; see entry) to raise an army to defend the fort, which would be called Fort Prince George. But Ange Duquesne de Menneville, marquis de Duquesne (1700–1778), the governor-general of New France, also planned to construct a fort at the same spot. He began preparing French troops to march southward and claim the area.

The French take the Forks while Washington struggles

Lieutenant Governor Dinwiddie promoted Washington to lieutenant colonel of the Virginia regiment and charged him with raising an army of two hundred men to defend Fort Prince George. Washington faced a difficult task in gathering and equipping an army to take into the Ohio Country, as the American colonists were not eager to support a war in the distant wilderness. Few men were willing to volunteer to serve in the army, and many farmers refused to provide food, horses, and wagons to supply the troops. Even after a month, Washington was only able to collect 150 men, eight subordinate officers, a few cannons, and some unsteady horses and wagons. When they left Alexandria, Virginia, on April 2, Washington's men did not have uniforms to wear or tents to protect them from the spring rains.

Washington's army made slow progress on their journey to the Forks. They chopped their way through the woods in order to clear the first road for wheeled vehicles through the Allegheny Mountains. It took them fifteen days to go just twenty miles.

In the meantime, one thousand French soldiers marched southward from New France. They reached the Forks (site of modern-day Pittsburgh, Pennsylvania) on April 17, while Washington was still crossing the Alleghenies. The commander of the French forces was Claude-Pierre Pecaudy, seigneur de Contrecoeur (1706–1775), a tough old veteran of the frontier service. Contrecoeur sent a messenger to the partially finished British fort at the Forks. He told the forty British soldiers and carpenters working there that they could either leave at once or be wiped out. The British abandoned

Fort Prince George, and the French proceeded to build their own fort, called Fort Duquesne.

A few days later, the small band of soldiers who had fled the unfinished British fort ran into Washington's advancing army. Washington was upset to hear that the French had captured Fort Prince George, but he soon began planning to reclaim the Forks. The retreating soldiers, who had seen the strength of the French forces with their own eyes, refused to join Washington and instead returned to Virginia. Washington continued on to an Ohio Company warehouse on the Monongahela River, about forty miles from the spot where the French were building Fort Duquesne. His men started building defenses in the area, which they called Red Stone Fort.

The assassination of Jumonville

From his position at the Forks, Contrecoeur followed Washington's progress closely through reports from Indian scouts. The French commander wanted to make sure that the British forces did not approach Fort Duquesne before it was finished. Since France and Great Britain had not declared war, however, Contrecoeur did not have the authority to launch an attack on Washington. Contrecoeur decided to send a messenger to meet with the British leader. He chose Joseph Coulon de Villiers de Jumonville (1718–1754), a young officer from a proud military family. Jumonville's mission was to

 People to Know

Benjamin Franklin (1706–1790): Wealthy and influential Philadelphia printer who unsuccessfully put forth a plan to unite the British colonies at the Albany Congress; later, he played important roles in the American Revolution and the drafting of the U.S. Constitution.

Claude-Pierre Pecaudy, seigneur de Contrecoeur (1706–1775): French military leader who captured the partially finished British fort at the Forks of the Ohio and established Fort Duquesne on the site.

Joseph Coulon de Villiers de Jumonville (1718–1754): French military leader who carried a message to Lieutenant Colonel George Washington, was attacked by Washington's forces, and murdered by Seneca tribe civil chief Tanaghrisson.

Tanaghrisson (?–1754): Seneca civil chief who murdered French diplomat Joseph Coulon de Villiers de Jumonville during Lieutenant Colonel George Washington's 1754 attack on French forces that started the French and Indian War.

George Washington (1732–1799): American military and political leader who took part in the early battles of the French and Indian War and went on to lead the American Revolution and serve as the first president of the United States.

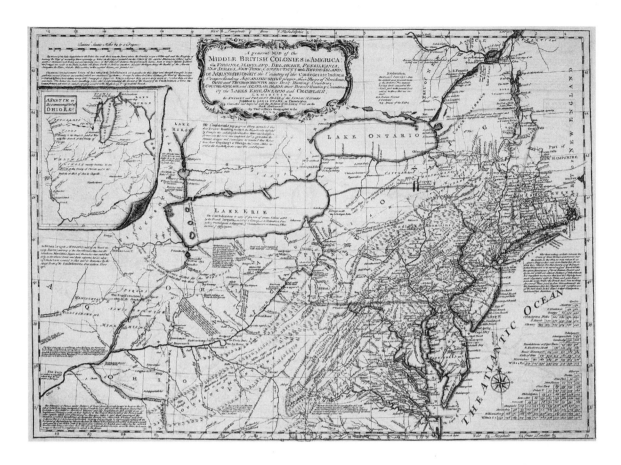

A 1758 map of the Ohio Valley and the surrounding area. *Reproduced by permission of the Corbis Corporation.*

gather information about Washington's plans and deliver a message warning him to leave the Ohio Country. Jumonville took along a small force of only about thirty-five men for his journey. He kept his groups small because he did not want to alarm Washington and provoke an attack.

As Jumonville's troops made their way toward Red Stone Fort, however, Washington learned from Indian scouts that there were French soldiers nearby. Fearing a sneak attack, Washington left the fort with a force of forty-seven men. This small army followed the Indian scout through the woods during a blinding rainstorm in order to meet with his chief, Tanaghrisson (?–1754; see box). Tanaghrisson, sometimes known as Half King, was a Seneca chief who represented the interests of the powerful Iroquois Confederacy in the Ohio Country. He supported the British because he hoped to stop the French from moving into the Ohio Country.

Tanaghrisson knew where the French troops under Jumonville had camped for the night. Washington moved his men, along with Tanaghrisson and a dozen of his warriors, into a circle surrounding the wooded hollow where the French were camped. In the early morning hours of May 28, Washington's forces attacked the French camp. The fighting lasted only about ten minutes before the French surrendered. Jumonville, who had been wounded along with several of his men, told Washington that he had come in peace to deliver a message. Several French and British soldiers gathered together and struggled to translate the message that Jumonville had been carrying.

According to Washington, Tanaghrisson suddenly stepped forward and murdered Jumonville by cracking his skull with a hatchet. Then Tanaghrisson's warriors joined in to kill and scalp the remaining French wounded. It took Washington a few moments to realize what was happening. By the time he regained control of the situation, ten French soldiers were dead. Washington quickly ordered his own troops to collect the remaining twenty-two French soldiers as prisoners and return to Red Stone Fort.

Historians have tried to explain this bloody event, which is regarded as the start of the French and Indian War (known in Europe as the Seven Years' War). They have pieced together evidence from several different eyewitness accounts. One account came from a French soldier named Monceau, who was part of Jumonville's army. Monceau escaped into the woods as Jumonville surrendered. He made his way to Fort Duquesne, where he told his commanders that Washington had launched a surprise attack and that the Indians did not take part in the fighting. A short time later, one of Tanaghrisson's warriors arrived at the French fort. He told the French commander that Washington's forces had murdered Jumonville and his men before their message had been translated. The warrior claimed that the British would have killed more French soldiers if Tanaghrisson had not stopped them.

But several other accounts support Washington's version of events. He claimed that his men had surprised the French forces in camp and began firing when the French went for their weapons. After the French surrendered, Wash-

Tanaghrisson, the Seneca Nation's "Half King"

Tanaghrisson is one of the more mysterious figures associated with the French and Indian War. The first historical mentions of this Indian leader date back to 1748, when the Iroquois Confederacy named him the leader of the Seneca and Delaware tribes that lived in the upper regions of the Ohio River Valley. Most leaders of the Iroquois Confederacy were known to their people as "king," but Tanaghrisson and the other Iroquois chiefs of the Ohio Country had only limited powers. They could negotiate with the French, the British, or other Indian leaders, and they were permitted to accept gifts on behalf of the Confederacy. But they were not allowed to make binding treaties or agreements without first obtaining the approval of the Confederacy's Grand Council leadership. As a result, Tanaghrisson became widely known as "Half King."

In the early 1750s, British traders ventured deep into the Ohio River Valley. Eager to make friends with Tanaghrisson, they gave him all sorts of gifts. Tanaghrisson was flattered by the presents, which he distributed to local village chiefs to ensure their continued loyalty to him. But Half King's relations with the British placed him out of step with other Indians. Many tribes in the region were leaning towards support of the French, who were also trying to establish themselves as the dominant European presence in the region.

In May 1754, Virginia's colonial leaders sent several hundred troops under the command of a young adventurer named George Washington (who would later became the first president of the United States) deep into the Ohio Country. When French forces at Fort Duquesne

ington said that Tanaghrisson attacked and killed Jumonville. Historians give several possible reasons for Tanaghrisson's murder of Jumonville. The Seneca chief had lost power with his people and was living as a refugee near the Forks with a small group of relatives and followers. Historians believe that Tanaghrisson may have felt that the only way to regain his position as a leader was by getting the British to help him move the French out of the Ohio Country. He murdered Jumonville—and then sent a messenger to the French claiming that Washington was responsible—in order to provoke the French and force them to retaliate against the British. According to this theory, the desperate chief started a war between the two European powers in a misguided attempt to protect his land and his people.

learned of Washington's approach, they sent a small force under the command of a young officer named Joseph Coulon de Villiers de Jumonville to warn him away.

When Tanaghrisson's warriors discovered that Jumonville's party was approaching, Half King led Washington to the site of their overnight camp. Encouraged by Tanaghrisson, Washington's men attacked the camp in the early hours of May 28. Jumonville surrendered after a short struggle. But when the French officer tried to explain to Washington that he had only been sent to deliver a message, Tanaghrisson stepped forward and buried a hatchet in Jumonville's skull. Tanaghrisson's warriors then massacred most of the remaining prisoners, to the stunned amazement of Washington. Today, Half King's murderous act is regarded as the opening chapter of the French and Indian War.

Tanaghrisson had hoped that Jumonville's death would further strengthen his relationship with the British and their colonial allies. But as the months passed, he decided that continuing relations with the British would be a mistake. Most other Indians in the Ohio Country preferred the French to the British, who were seen as a much greater threat to their villages and hunting grounds. With this in mind, Half King gathered his family and left for a frontier trading post at Aughwick (now Shirleysburg, Pennsylvania). Shortly after his arrival, he was struck down by a terrible sickness. His family and followers blamed his illness on witchcraft. Tanaghrisson died of this mysterious sickness on October 4, 1754.

Washington defeated at Fort Necessity

The French and British viewpoints differed on the battle that had taken place on May 28. The French believed Jumonville's death was the murder of a diplomat, and they planned to take revenge on the British. But the British thought Jumonville was a spy, and said Washington was justified in attacking him. Shortly after word of the battle reached the British colonies, Washington was promoted to colonel of the Virginia regiment and received two hundred reinforcements (fresh troops). He decided to collect some Indian allies and launch an attack upon Fort Duquesne. He started out by marching his troops toward Red Stone Fort in preparation for the attack.

George Washington (center, holding sword) meets with others to discuss the possibility of a surrender to the French in 1754.

Reproduced by permission of the Corbis Corporation.

Meanwhile, French leaders at the Forks sent a force of eight hundred soldiers and four hundred Indian allies to attack Washington. The commander of the French troops was Captain Louis Coulon de Villiers (1710–1757), the older brother of Jumonville. When an Indian scout told Washington that the French were approaching his position, the young colonel decided to retreat and meet the French at Fort Necessity. Fort Necessity was a small circular fort made of split logs. It was located in a grassy meadow surrounded by wooded hills. By the time Washington's troops reached the fort, they were tired and ill from carrying their supplies back and forth to Red Stone Fort. In fact, only three hundred of his four hundred men were healthy enough to fight. Sensing defeat, his Indian allies abandoned their posts and slipped away into the woods. Washington only had time to dig a shallow trench around the fort before the French arrived.

The battle began on July 3, 1754. The French forces had the advantage from the start. They were able to hide behind trees and angle their musket fire downhill into the fort and the trench that surrounded it. Washington's troops were hit badly. To make matters worse for the British, a heavy rainstorm ruined the ammunition and gunpowder that was stored in the fort. By that evening, one hundred of Washington's men had been killed or wounded.

The French asked Washington to send a messenger out of the fort to discuss terms of surrender. Washington sent his old friend Jacob van Braam, a Dutchman who had served as a translator on an earlier mission. To Washington's surprise, the French conditions for his surrender seemed quite generous. The French offered to allow his men to march out of the fort and return to Virginia, taking their guns and all the possessions they could carry on their backs. In exchange, he only had to sign a paper admitting his responsibility in the death of Jumonville.

But the French forces had good reasons for setting Washington and his men free. Washington did not know that the French troops were running low on ammunition and supplies at that time. They were also worried that the British would soon receive reinforcements. Finally, the French commander was not sure whether he was allowed to take prisoners since France and Great Britain had not yet declared war.

Mistakes threaten Washington's career

As it turned out, the terms of surrender were more complicated than Washington realized. The rain-soaked paper that he signed said that he was responsible for the "assassination" of Jumonville. Van Braam had mistakenly translated the French word "assassination" as "death." This misunderstanding damaged the young colonel's reputation. Washington had been willing to admit that Jumonville had been killed in his presence by Indians who were supposed to be under his command, but he was horrified to discover that he had signed a confession of murder. French newspapers published the document and used it to create feelings of anger and resentment toward the British.

Washington and his troops began their march back to Virginia on July 4. As they left Fort Necessity, they were shocked to see that some of the Indians who had been fighting alongside the French were former British allies. In fact, many of the tribes in the Ohio Country felt that Washington had used poor judgment in the battle. His defeat convinced them to support the French. They recognized that they were caught in the middle of the fight between France and Great Britain, so they wanted to support whichever side was more likely to emerge the winner.

As soon as Washington's forces moved out of the area, the French burned down Fort Necessity and Red Stone Fort, thereby removing all traces of British military presence from the Ohio Country. When Washington arrived back in Virginia, some supporters claimed that he was a hero for standing up to the French when he was outnumbered. Others claimed that Washington's mistakes had allowed the French to take control of the Ohio Country.

By this time, it had become clear that France and Great Britain were going to enter into a war over their North American territories. Washington thought his Virginia regiment would become part of the regular British Army and that he would be promoted to colonel. But British leaders felt Washington and his colonial army had embarrassed them. They refused to offer Washington a commission in the British Army, so he resigned from the military.

The Albany Congress

At the same time as Washington was fighting at Fort Necessity, colonial leaders were holding an important meeting in Albany, New York. This meeting, known as the Albany Congress, had two main goals. One goal was to improve relations between the colonies and the Iroquois Confederacy, a powerful alliance of six Indian (Native American) nations. The second was to establish a unified approach for defending the frontier against French advances.

At this point in time, the thirteen British colonies in North America were largely independent. They competed with one another for land and power, but were unified in their loyalty to Great Britain. The distrust and lack of cooperation between the colonies helps explain why Washington had trouble raising an army to fight in the Ohio Country. Dinwiddie asked other colonies to send troops, but they thought that by helping Washington they would be helping Virginia expand its territory. The colony of New York had a similar experience at the Albany Congress. New York, which shared its northern border with New France, asked the other colonies to contribute money and troops to help it build forts to protect this border. But the other colonies were interested only in protecting their own borders.

The Albany Congress brought together a group of colonial leaders, including the wealthy and influential Philadelphia printer Benjamin Franklin (1706–1790), to address the lack of cooperation between colonies. Franklin argued that the colonies could be a powerful part of the British empire if they worked together. But if they remained separate, he claimed that they were weak and could be conquered by France, one by one. He came up with a Plan of Union, known as the Albany Plan, that would have created a single government for all the British colonies in America. Each colony would send representatives to this government, which would be led by a British governor-general. The colonial government would take charge of issues that affected all the colonies, such as Indian relations, westward expansion, and defense.

Philadelphia printer and future American statesman Benjamin Franklin proposed the Albany Plan, which would have created one government for the British colonies in America. *Courtesy of the Library of Congress.*

The individual colonies wanted to remain independent, though, so none of them approved the Albany Plan. Historians doubt that the British government would have accepted the plan anyway, because British leaders did not want the colonies to gain too much power. But the Albany Congress did help British leaders understand that the colonies were not willing to band together to defend themselves against France. Instead, Great Britain would be forced to send its own armies and military leaders to North America. The government sent two British Army regiments to the colonies and appointed a

British general, **Edward Braddock** (1695–1755; see entry), as commander in chief. Braddock would take charge of all British and colonial forces during the war against France.

The Albany Congress also convinced the British government to intervene in the relations between the colonies and the Iroquois Confederacy. Although the meeting was supposed to help improve relations between the colonies and the Indians, it actually created more hard feelings and distrust. Representatives from the Connecticut and Pennsylvania colonies spent much of the time bribing or tricking the Indians into giving up their land. The Iroquois representatives expressed anger at both the French and the British for trying to claim their rightful territory, but they finally agreed to renew their alliance with the British. After the meeting ended, British leaders appointed **William Johnson** (1715–1774; see entry) as their Indian representative and gave him sole authority to negotiate future military alliances and land treaties with the tribes.

1755: British Forces Suffer a Serious Defeat

4

British leaders in London were shocked to hear about the defeat of American military leader **George Washington** (1732–1799; see entry) at Fort Necessity. Although some of them did not want to enter the French and Indian War (known in Europe as the Seven Years' War), others were determined to expand British land holdings in North America by removing the French from the Ohio Country. But Washington's defeat had convinced them that the American colonists were no match for the French. They decided to send an experienced British general and two regiments of well-trained British soldiers to carry out their plans.

Major General **Edward Braddock** (1695–1755; see entry), who arrived in America in early 1755, carried orders from King George II (1683–1760) of England. These orders named Braddock commander-in-chief of all British and American armed forces and gave him full responsibility for organizing the defense of the colonies. French leaders in Paris soon learned about the British plans. In response, they decided to send thousands of French troops across the Atlantic Ocean to help defend their colonies in New France. They also began se-

Acadians: French-speaking Catholic residents of Nova Scotia who were deported when the British captured the region in 1755.

Irregulars: Soldiers who were not part of the formal British Army, including troops and militia recruited in the American colonies; irregulars tended to have less military training and poorer equipment than British regulars.

Ohio Country: A vast wilderness that stretched from the Great Lakes in the north to the Ohio River in the South, and from the Allegheny Mountains in the east to the Mississippi River in the west; the French and British fought for control of this region, which lay between the French and British colonies in North America.

Regulars: Professional soldiers of the British Army; they tended to be highly trained and well equipped compared to irregulars from the American colonies.

cret negotiations with Austria to end its alliance with Great Britain. If successful, this move would shift the balance of power in Europe toward France.

Braddock takes charge

A blunt and arrogant officer, Braddock felt that his position as commander-in-chief gave him power over the colonial governors, and he began issuing orders as soon as he arrived in North America. For example, he announced that he was setting up a common defense fund to support his military operations and that he expected all of the colonies to contribute money to it. He also informed the colonial governors that they were to provide supplies, quarters, and transportation for his forces, as well as additional soldiers from their colonial militias. This caused a problem with the Pennsylvania Assembly, which was controlled by members of the Quaker religion. Because Quakers are pacifists (believers in nonviolence), the Assembly refused to send money to support Braddock's army. Braddock responded by threatening to use some of his forces against Pennsylvania.

In April 1755, the general called a meeting of all the colonial governors. He started the session by scolding the governors for not delivering the money and supplies he wanted. Then Braddock outlined his ambitious plans for pushing the French out of the Ohio Country and defending the American colonies. These plans, which had been designed by British leaders in London, involved four military actions that were supposed to take place at the same time. First, Braddock and his two regiments of British soldiers would attack Fort Duquesne, the French stronghold at the Forks of the Ohio. Second, two regiments under Massachusetts governor William

Shirley (1694–1771) would seize the French fort at Niagara on Lake Ontario. Third, **William Johnson** (1715–1774; see entry) and a mixed regiment of colonial soldiers and Mohawk warriors would attack Fort St. Frédéric, located at Crown Point on Lake Champlain (in the northeastern corner of modern New York State). Fourth, an expedition of colonial soldiers from Boston would capture Fort Beauséjour in Nova Scotia (on the Atlantic coast of modern Canada).

Braddock's plans surprised and alarmed the colonial governors. They noticed a number of flaws that could create serious problems for the armies involved. For example, the British leaders who developed the plans did not seem to understand wilderness conditions. Braddock and his two regiments planned to follow the road Washington had cut through the Allegheny Mountains to get to Fort Duquesne from Virginia. But this road was rough and narrow, and would need a great deal of work before it could be used by wagons hauling heavy artillery. The other expeditions planned to use boats to transport men and supplies to their target forts on rivers. But these rivers had wide variations in water levels and were often choked with fallen trees.

British planners also expected the colonies to contribute enough money and supplies to support all four military campaigns. But this placed a great deal of strain on the limited resources of the colonies. As a result, the commanders of the four expeditions had to compete for soldiers, boats, wagons, guns, clothing, shelter, and other supplies. The expeditions thus became more expensive, took longer to prepare, and had lower chances for success.

People to Know

Edward Braddock (1695–1755): British military leader who served as commander-in-chief of British forces in North America in 1755 and was killed in a disastrous early battle on the Monongahela River.

Baron Ludwig August (also known as Jean-Armand) Dieskau (1701–1767): French military leader who lost the Battle of Lake George and was wounded and captured by the British.

William Johnson (1715–1774): British general who served as chief of Indian affairs and won the Battle of Lake George.

William Shirley (1694–1771): Governor of Massachusetts who served as commander-in-chief of British forces in North America following the death of Edward Braddock.

George Washington (1732–1799): American military and political leader who took part in the early battles of the French and Indian War and went on to lead the American Revolution and serve as the first president of the United States.

British major general Edward Braddock. *Courtesy of the Library of Congress.*

The colonial governors tried to tell Braddock about the flaws in his plan. They insisted that they could not provide all the men and supplies Braddock was requesting. They came up with several ideas about how to change his plans to make them work better. Instead of launching four expeditions at the same time, for example, they suggested that he concentrate his efforts on capturing the French fort at Niagara. This would isolate Fort Duquesne and other forts in the Ohio Country, preventing them from receiving troops and supplies. When Braddock rejected this idea, the governors suggested that Braddock start his march to Fort Duquesne from Pennsylvania instead of Virginia. This would cut the length of his journey and allow his troops to travel on an improved road. But Braddock refused to listen to this idea as well. He insisted on following his orders exactly as they were written by the king and other British leaders.

Braddock's forces advance toward Fort Duquesne

Just as the governors had warned, Braddock faced a number of delays in getting the supplies he needed. On May 29, 1755, he finally began marching toward Fort Duquesne with twenty-two hundred men. Most of these men were "regular" soldiers with the British Army. They wore fancy uniforms with bright red coats and considered themselves well-trained, professional soldiers. Braddock's army also included one hundred "irregular" soldiers from the Virginia militia, as well as some engineers and frontiersmen to improve the road and serve as guides. The irregular soldiers were not part of the formal British Army, and generally had less military training and poorer equipment than the regular soldiers. Another

member of Braddock's army was George Washington, who had asked to join because he hoped to learn from the experienced British general. Washington's knowledge of the wilderness would give the troops an advantage they would not otherwise have, and Braddock welcomed him as a volunteer aide on his staff.

Braddock's forces made slow progress over the 120 miles to Fort Duquesne. As they lugged heavy artillery and wagons full of supplies through the mountains—cutting down trees and blasting huge boulders to clear the road as they went—they sometimes advanced only two miles per day. As he rode along with Braddock, Washington learned that his commanding officer knew very little about wilderness warfare. The general expected to meet the enemy on a field of battle, where his men could form rows and take turns firing and reloading. But Washington knew that the French and their Indian (Native American) allies were more likely to use surprise ambushes and to fire from behind cover of rocks and

Edward Braddock leads his British forces towards Fort Duquesne in Pennsylvania in 1755. *Reproduced by permission of Getty Images.*

Robert Stobo, Daring British Prisoner of War

Robert Stobo was born in Glasgow, Scotland, in 1727. He immigrated to the American colonies as a young man and settled in Virginia, where he became a prosperous merchant. Stobo was a captain in the Virginia militia at the time the French and Indian War began. In fact, he accompanied George Washington's troops into the Ohio Country in 1754.

Stobo was taken hostage by the French following the British defeat in the Battle of Fort Necessity. He initially was held at Fort Duquesne as a prisoner of war. Stobo secretly created a detailed map of the fort and smuggled it out with visiting Indians. The Indians delivered the map to Washington as British forces under General Edward Braddock approached Fort Duquesne in 1755.

After Braddock's forces suffered a terrible defeat, however, the French discovered Stobo's map among Braddock's captured papers. The French then sent Stobo to Quebec and put him on trial for treason (betraying the country). He was sentenced to be executed on November 8, 1755, but the sentence was never carried out because the king never approved the execution.

Stobo remained in Quebec for the next four years. He spent some of this time in prison, but as the years passed he made friends in the city and was allowed more freedom. Stobo finally escaped in the spring of 1759 and made a dangerous

trees. Washington tried to tell Braddock about frontier conditions and prepare him for the way the French and Indians would fight. But the general insisted that his plans would work because they had always worked in previous wars.

At one point in their journey, Braddock and his army met a group of Indians led by Shingas, an Ohio Delaware war chief. Shingas explained that he and his warriors had been sent by William Johnson—the official British representative to the Indians—to assist Braddock. Shingas said that he was willing to help the British because he wanted to get the French out of the Ohio Country. He showed his good intentions by giving Braddock a detailed map of Fort Duquesne. This map had been prepared by Captain Robert Stobo (1727–c. 1772; see box), a British officer who had been held prisoner at the fort since Washington's defeat at Fort Necessity. Shingas had smuggled the map out of the French fort at journey down the St. Lawrence River to Louisbourg. There he joined the British forces that were preparing to attack Quebec. Stobo served in the army of General **James Wolfe** (1727–1759; see entry) and supposedly pointed out the cove where Wolfe launched his successful attack on the French city.

Once the British forces captured Quebec, Stobo returned to Virginia. He received official thanks from the colonial government and a monetary reward. He also received a promotion from the army along with his back pay for the years he was held prisoner. Stobo rejoined the army and served in Canada, the West Indies, and England through 1770. Then his name disappears from army records, and it is unclear what happened to him.

In 1767, Stobo had purchased land on Lake Champlain in New York with the intention of settling there. He had also received a land bounty of nine thousand acres on the Ohio River (in what is now West Virginia) for his military service. Washington tried repeatedly to find Stobo so that he could purchase Stobo's land claims, but he never located the former captain. Historians suspect that Stobo died in England, New York, or West Virginia around 1772. His wartime adventures were captured in the book *Memoirs of Major Robert Stobo of the Virginia Regiment*, published in 1800.

great danger to himself. In exchange for their help, Shingas and his warriors asked for Braddock's word that British settlers would share the Ohio Country with them and become their partners in trade. But Braddock felt that his army did not need any help from the Indians. He offended Shingas by telling him that the British planned to control the Ohio Country and use it in any way they wished. Shingas and his warriors left. Eventually, they and most other Indians joined the French forces.

As Braddock's army continued its slow progress, Washington warned the general that the French might have time to send reinforcements to the fort. Braddock agreed to send twelve hundred troops ahead as an advance party, while the remaining troops followed with the heavy artillery. Washington became ill and had to stay with the rear group for a while. But he caught up with Braddock and the advance party near the Monongahela River, about twelve miles from Fort Duquesne. The British forces crossed the river on July 9 and planned to make their assault on the fort the following day.

The French officer in charge of Fort Duquesne, Claude-Pierre Pecaudy, seigneur de Contrecoeur (1706–1775), followed the progress of Braddock's army through reports from scouts. Contrecoeur had sixteen hundred men defending the fort, including French army, Canadian militia, and Indian warriors. The fort itself was small, however, and only two hundred men could fit inside. Contrecoeur decided that his best chance for victory would be to launch a surprise attack before Braddock's army reached the fort. On July 9, Contrecoeur sent half of his men to attack the British forces. The French troops, which were led by Captain Daniel Lienard de Beaujeu (1711–1755), included over six hundred Indians. They were well armed, but they were able to move quickly because they did not carry many other supplies. Compared to their enemies, they were also well rested, well fed, and familiar with the woods and the tactics of wilderness warfare.

Disaster on the Monongahela

The French and British forces ran into each other somewhat suddenly. At the front of the long line of British troops were three hundred regulars under Lieutenant Colonel Thomas Gage (1719–1787). Beaujeu led the French forces, followed by his Indian warriors. As the two sides exchanged musket fire, Beaujeu was killed within minutes. Then the French and Indians rushed forward into the cover of the woods and continued firing, while the British troops remained in the road and tried to fight in formation. The neat rows of bright red coats made perfect targets for the French and Indians hiding behind trees, and they were able to kill many British soldiers. In fact, fifteen of the eighteen officers in Gage's company were killed in the early stages of the battle. The British troops tried to return fire, but they had little success because they could barely see the enemy in the forest.

With their officers and fellow soldiers falling all around them, the remaining British troops finally retreated in panic. A short distance up the road, they ran into the main column of soldiers, led by General Braddock. As noted in his journal, Washington recalled that he and the general ordered the terrified men to halt "with as much success ... as if we had attempted to have stopped the wild bears of the mountains." The main column of soldiers soon came under attack as well, from Indians hiding in the woods. The British army had been trained to fight in formation, so the men huddled together in the road and returned fire as best they could. Braddock and his officers rode around on horseback trying to rally and organize the troops, but the men were too confused and frightened to follow orders. At one point, Washington asked Braddock for permission to lead the colonial soldiers into the woods to fight in the same way as the enemy, but the general refused.

Braddock was eventually shot in the back and lost consciousness. Washington had two horses shot out from under him—and bullet holes in his coat and hat—but managed to escape injury. As one of the only officers left among the British forces, Washington led their retreat across the Monongahela River. They left behind about nine hundred British soldiers who had been killed or wounded in the three-hour battle, including sixty-three of eighty-six officers. Many of these men were scalped (a bloody Indian war ritual in which warriors used a sharp knife to cut the scalps off of people they had conquered) by the triumphant Indians. When Braddock regained consciousness, he ordered Washington to ride back forty miles to bring up reinforcements from the rear.

Washington was exhausted from the battle and remained weak from his illness, but he somehow managed to carry out the order. In fact, he sometimes crawled on his hands and knees to find the road through the dark woods. To make matters worse, he passed many wounded soldiers who were struggling to drag themselves away from the battle scene. "The dead—the dying—the groans—lamentation [wailing]—and cries along the road of the wounded for help ... were enough to pierce a heart of adamant [stone]," he re-

Edward Braddock and his men are ambushed by French and Indian troops near Fort Duquesne in the Ohio Country. *Reproduced by permission of Getty Images.*

A French Soldier Recalls Braddock's Defeat

The following excerpt is taken from the journal of Jolicoeur Charles Bonin, a young Frenchman who traveled through the French colonies in North America between 1751 and 1761. During this time, he served with the French military and took part in several battles of the French and Indian War. In this passage, he describes General Edward Braddock's defeat on the Monongahela River from the point of view of a French soldier.

On the morning of July 9th the march [of French and Indian forces from Fort Duquesne] was begun.... The army marched through the woods in three columns to meet the enemy [British and American forces under Braddock], with our scouts always in the advance. At noon, the army halted when the news came that part of the enemy's army, with its artillery had crossed the river, and had halted to await

the rear guard and the baggage train. We were then only a quarter league [about one mile] from them. Immediately the order was given to advance in double-quick time, and to attack the enemy simultaneously from the front and both flanks. This order was hastily carried out. The savages [Indians] shouted their war cry, and the French opened fire with a volley [round], which was followed by a volley by the savages. The enemy, taken by surprise, formed a line of battle, and fired their artillery. [Captain Daniel Lienard] De Beaujeu [commander of the French and Indian forces] was killed by the first volley; and the savages, terrified by the unfamiliar noise of the cannon, took flight momentarily. But Captain [Jean-Daniel] Dumas took command immediately after Sieur de Beaujeu's death, and encouraged the French. The savages saw the steadfastness of the Frenchmen and no longer heard the cannon, which the French had seized. They,

membered in his journal. "The gloom and horror ... was not a little increased by the impervious [impossible to penetrate] darkness occasioned by the close shade of thick woods."

By the time Washington reached the other half of Braddock's army, they had already heard about the battle. The men were too frightened to follow Washington's orders and instead began to retreat. Washington returned to the advance guard and organized their retreat. Braddock died on July 13, on the journey back to Virginia. His remaining officers buried him in an unmarked grave and ran their wagons over it so the Indians would not find it.

Braddock takes the blame

People in the colonies were shocked to hear about the defeat of Braddock's army. Many people blamed Braddock and *therefore, returned to charge the enemy, following the French example, and forced them to retreat after two hours of fierce combat.... The English hastily crossed the river, where many were killed by the never-ending hail of bullets upon them. In his flight, the enemy lost artillery, baggage train, and fifteen flags, as well as the military chest [a trunk containing important documents].... General Braddock was wounded in the battle, and taken away by the fugitives [fleeing soldiers] in a coach [stagecoach], which was with the rear guard on the other side of the river. It was indeed a fancy article, absolutely useless in the forest and mountains where it was the first one ever to be seen....*

Once the British retreated, the French and Indian forces moved across the battlefield, destroying the British cannons, emptying the military chest of money and documents, and searching the bodies of dead soldiers for valuables. Bonin ends his discussion of the battle by criticizing Braddock's performance.

General Braddock made the same mistake as Baron Dieskau [the French general who lost the Battle of Lake George] by arranging his troops in formal battle order in the middle of the forest. In this way, they could not make an effective attack, and ran the risk of being overcome, as did happen. This was the opinion of the French Canadians, from which it may be concluded that it is wiser to use the fighting methods of the country you are in.

Source: Bonin, Jolicoeur Charles. Memoir of a French and Indian War Soldier. *Edited by Andrew Gallup. Bowie, MD: Heritage Books, 1993. First published as* Voyage au Canada, dans le nord de l'Amérique Septentrionale, depuis l'an 1751 à 1761, par J. C. B. *Quebec: Abbé H. R. Casgrain, 1887.*

said that he should have known that the European style of fighting in formation would not work in the North American wilderness. In fact, this criticism led to a general feeling in the colonies that American irregular troops were better suited to this new brand of warfare than British regulars. Some historians also place the blame on Braddock. They admit that he was brave during the battle, but they also note that he lost even though he had a larger army and better weapons than the enemy. Another factor in Braddock's defeat was his rejection of Indian help. In contrast, Contrecoeur and other French leaders understood the need for Indian cooperation and worked hard to establish good relations with the tribes. Overall, the terrible defeat ruined Braddock's reputation.

At the same time, however, George Washington emerged from the battle as a hero. He was praised for his bravery throughout the colonies, and his reputation soared.

The wounded Edward Braddock is carried away by his retreating troops. The fallen general died soon thereafter. *Reproduced by permission of Getty Images.*

In fact, one preacher expressed the opinion that Washington had survived the battle because he was destined to provide some great service to his country. For his part, Washington never criticized Braddock. Instead, he blamed the defeat on the troops who ran from danger and refused to follow orders.

Braddock's defeat worried the people of the Virginia, Pennsylvania, and Maryland colonies. They thought that the French and Indians might use the road Braddock built to march east and attack them. Adding to these fears, the settlers along the western frontier of these colonies increasingly fell victim to Indian raids as more tribes from the Ohio Country joined forces with the French. In fact, one hundred Virginians had been killed or taken captive by the fall of 1755. Many others abandoned their homesteads and returned east to more populated areas. In response to these threats, the colonies raised a thousand-man regiment and made Washington its colonel. He spent the next two years defending the Virginia frontier against Indian attacks.

British capture Nova Scotia and deport the Acadians

Braddock's death left William Shirley—the governor of Massachusetts Colony who had been selected to lead the British assault on the French fort at Niagara—in charge of all the British forces in North America. But Shirley was a political leader who had very little military experience, so he felt anxious about taking command. As Braddock had been moving his troops through the mountains and fighting along the Monongahela, Shirley's Niagara expedition and William Johnson's Crown Point expedition had been competing for men and supplies in Albany. In the meantime, thousands of French reinforcements had arrived in Canada by ship despite the attempts of the British Navy to stop them. Faced with increasing levels of responsibility and decreasing chances of success, Shirley decided to wait until the following spring to move against Niagara.

The four-part British plan did achieve one of its goals during the summer of 1755. In June, a few weeks before Braddock's defeat, colonial forces out of Boston succeeded in capturing Fort Beauséjour in Nova Scotia. The French and British had been fighting for control of Nova Scotia, a peninsula of land that extends into the Atlantic Ocean north of present-day Maine, ever since King George's War (1743–48). The French had built Fort Beauséjour on the narrow section of land that connects Nova Scotia to the Canadian mainland in 1750. The British had responded by building Fort Lawrence a few miles away, on the other side of the Missaguash River.

The idea of controlling Nova Scotia was very popular among Americans who lived in the crowded New England colonies. If Great Britain took over the region, they figured there would be an abundance of new land to settle. This attitude made it easy to raise two regiments of New England soldiers to attack Fort Beauséjour. Using Fort Lawrence as a base, these forces set up artillery and began shelling the French fort. One of the first artillery shells they fired killed half a dozen French officers as they sat down to breakfast. Once their leaders were killed, the French soldiers holding the fort surrendered quickly. The British took control of Fort Beauséjour and renamed it Fort Cumberland.

At the time the British took control of Nova Scotia, the region had been the home of French-speaking Catholics

Longfellow Describes the Acadian Tragedy in "Evangeline"

American poet Henry Wadsworth Longfellow (1807–1882) used the tragic story of the Acadians as the background for his famous poem "Evangeline." The Acadians were French-speaking Catholics who were forced to leave their homes when the British took control of Nova Scotia during the French and Indian War. Thousands of Acadians were loaded onto British ships and transported down the Atlantic coast to the American colonies. Small groups were dropped off in coastal cities from New Hampshire to North Carolina. Since the Acadians spoke a different language and practiced a different religion from the colonists, they remained outsiders and suffered many hardships. Some Acadians eventually made their way back to Canada, while others migrated to French-speaking settlements in the Caribbean islands or in Louisiana, where they became known as Cajuns.

Longfellow's poem centers around the fictional character of Evangeline, a gentle seventeen-year-old beauty who is the daughter of one of Acadia's wealthiest farmers. Evangeline loves Gabriel, the son of the respected blacksmith in the village of Grand-Pre. Evangeline leads a happy life in her peaceful village until the British arrive and take over Nova Scotia. A short time later, she and the other villagers are herded onto British ships. In the confusion, Evangeline and Gabriel are separated. The rest

known as Acadians for several generations. The new British governor of Nova Scotia, Charles Lawrence (1709–1760), viewed the Acadians as a dangerous threat. Since the Acadians refused to take an oath of loyalty to the king of England, Lawrence believed they must secretly be helping the French. He worried that they might start a rebellion and attack British settlers who moved into the region. To avoid such trouble, Lawrence decided to deport (remove from the country by force) the Acadians.

The operation began in September 1755. Over six thousand Acadians were packed onto ships and transported to the American colonies. Thousands of others fled into the woods or to mainland Canada to avoid being deported. The ships stopped at many ports along the Atlantic coast, dropping off a few dozen Acadians in each city. Since the Acadians spoke a different language and practiced a different religion from the American colonists, they had trouble fitting in, and suffered of the poem describes Evangeline's difficult life in America and her struggles to find her beloved Gabriel.

In the following excerpt from "Evangeline," Longfellow describes the emptiness of the land, now that the people who had lived there for generations are gone. He compares the Acadians to autumn leaves that have been scattered by the wind:

> This is the forest primeval [ancient]; but where are the hearts that beneath it
>
> Leaped like the roe [deer], when he hears in the woodland the voice of the huntsman?
>
> Where is the thatch-roofed village, the home of Acadian farmers—
>
> Men whose lives glided on like rivers that water the woodlands,
>
> Darkened by shadows of earth, but reflecting an image of heaven?
>
> Waste [destroyed] are those pleasant farms, and the farmers forever departed!
>
> Scattered like dust and leaves, when the mighty blasts of October
>
> Seize them, and whirl them aloft, and sprinkle them far o'er [over] the ocean.
>
> Naught [nothing] but tradition remains of the beautiful village of Grand-Pre.

Source: Longfellow, Henry Wadsworth. Evangeline. Holicong, PA: Wildside Press, 2002. Poem written in 1847.

many hardships. Most of the transplanted Acadians moved on within a few years. Some returned to Canada, while others ended up in French-speaking settlements in the West Indies. A large group of Acadians migrated to New Orleans, where their ancestors became known by the shortened name Cajuns.

Many historians have criticized the British for their treatment of the Acadians. In his book *Crucible of War,* Fred Anderson compared the deportation of the Acadians to modern "ethnic cleansing" operations, in which members of a certain racial or religious group try to get rid of all the people in their country who come from different backgrounds. Anderson and others have claimed that the main reason British authorities deported the Acadians was to make room for their own settlers to form colonies in Nova Scotia. In fact, five thousand British settlers had moved to Nova Scotia by 1763, and some of them took over the farms and homesteads that once belonged to the Acadians.

Acadians are rounded up by the British and moved from Nova Scotia in 1765.

Reproduced by permission of the Corbis Corporation.

Johnson wins the Battle of Lake George

The last part of Braddock's plan finally got underway in September 1755, when colonial and Indian forces under William Johnson began moving toward Fort St. Frédéric on Lake Champlain. Like Shirley, Johnson was unsure about his skills as a general and was not eager to go into battle. Johnson had struggled for months to train his thirty-five hundred troops, build or hire boats, and transport cannons and other supplies to Lake George, which would serve as the launching point for his expedition. To be safe, he also decided to build a British fort on the Hudson River, called Fort Edward, before he attacked the French fort.

The French officer in charge of Fort St. Frédéric was Baron Ludwig August (also known as Jean-Armand) Dieskau (1701–1767). Dieskau had three thousand men to defend the fort. After receiving reports from scouts about British preparations, Dieskau decided to attack Fort Edward. The British fort

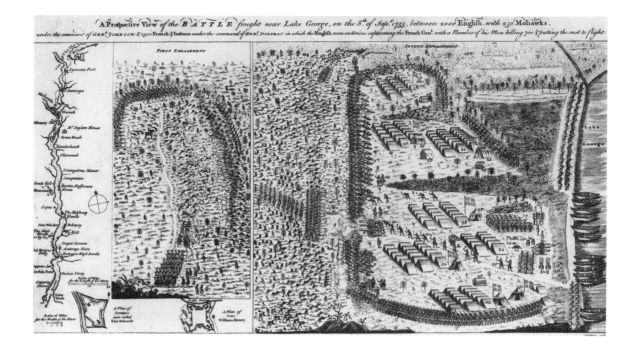

A Prospective View of the BATTLE fought near Lake George, on the 8.th of Sept.r 1755, between 2000 English, with 250 Mohawks. under the command of GEN.l JOHNSON & 2500 French & Indians under the command of GEN.l DIESKAU in which the English were victorious captivating the French Gen.l with a Number of his Men killing 700 & putting the rest to flight.

A map showing the positions of the soldiers during the Battle of Lake George in September 1755. *Reproduced by permission of Getty Images.*

was only partially completed and lightly defended at this time. Dieskau hoped to destroy the boats, cannons, and other supplies stored there so the British could not use them in an attack against Fort St. Frédéric. If he was successful in capturing Fort Edward, Dieskau might be able to roll back the British defenses all the way to Albany.

Dieskau took a force of fifteen hundred men—including about two hundred regular French Army soldiers, six hundred irregular Canadian militia soldiers, and seven hundred Indian warriors—to attack Fort Edward. By early September, the French and Indian forces had advanced to the strategic spot where Lake George and Lake Champlain meet, known as Carillon by the French and Ticonderoga by the British. As they neared Fort Edward, however, the Indians told Dieskau that they were not willing to attack a fixed defensive position like the fort. Unable to change the warriors' minds, Dieskau decided to attack Johnson's camp on Lake George instead.

In the meantime, Johnson's Mohawk scouts told the general that the French were nearing Fort Edward. Johnson immediately sent one thousand colonial troops and two hundred Mohawk warriors from his camp to help defend the fort.

Two Indians are captured by British soldiers during the French and Indian War.
Reproduced by permission of the Corbis Corporation.

The French and British forces ran into each other a short distance from Johnson's camp on the morning of September 8. The American colonial soldiers lacked the strict discipline and training of the British regulars. Instead of standing still and fighting in formation, they fought from cover in the woods as they retreated back toward their camp. Johnson's remaining men heard the shots in the distance and quickly strengthened the camp's defenses.

The French and Indian forces chased the British back to the camp on Lake George. At this point, however, the Indians once again refused to attack an enemy stronghold. The Canadian troops took their cue from the Indians and stopped fighting as well. Hoping to shame his irregular forces into attacking, Dieskau ordered his two hundred French regulars to storm the British defenses. This turned out to be a terrible mistake, as the French soldiers were cut down by cannon and musket fire long before they reached the enemy. Dieskau was wounded and eventually captured by the British.

The French and Indian forces soon retreated back into the woods. About four hundred men stopped to rest near the original site of the battle. They did not realize that two hundred British colonial troops were approaching their position from the other direction. British leaders at Fort Edward had heard the battle and sent these forces to help Johnson. The colonials launched a surprise attack on the disorganized French and Indian forces and killed or captured nearly all of them.

The British had won the battle, which came to be known as the Battle of Lake George. Johnson was hailed as a hero, even though his expedition had failed even to approach Fort St. Frédéric. The French remained in control of Lake Champlain and built another fort at Carillon (Ticonderoga) at the north end of Lake George. The British did not advance any further and instead built a fort at the south end of Lake George, called Fort William Henry, to protect the road to Albany.

1756–57: The French Gain the Upper Hand

5

By the time France formally declared war on Great Britain in 1756, the two European powers and their allies had already been fighting in the North American wilderness for two years. The declaration of war marked the beginning of a second phase of the conflict. The French and Indian War, as it was known in North America, spread to Europe and to other French and British colonies around the world. It even gained a new name in Europe—the Seven Years' War.

Events in Europe

Before the French and Indian War, the nations of Europe had formed fairly stable alliances that created a balance of power. Great Britain's allies included Holland and Austria, while France was allied with Prussia (a country containing modern-day Germany and parts of Poland and Russia). In 1756, however, these alliances were turned upside-down. France secretly negotiated an alliance with Austria, while Great Britain made a similar deal with Prussia.

A few weeks after declaring war on Great Britain, France captured a British military base on the Mediterranean island of Minorca. The British responded by taking control of a French factory in India. But the real battles of the European war began in August 1756, when King Frederick II (1712–1786) of Prussia launched military operations against Austria. France had signed a treaty in which it promised to defend Austria. By mid-1757, France had helped its ally turn back the invasion and Prussia withdrew from Austria. Following his defeat, however, King Frederick faced threats from France, Sweden, and Russia.

British leaders could not send troops to help Prussia because their forces were busy in North America or conducting naval operations along the French coast. But Great Britain did provide King Frederick with money that helped him defeat the French in the Battle of Rossbach in November. Prussia claimed another victory over Austria in Silesia in December. By the end of 1757, the European war had turned in Great Britain's favor as France was forced to abandon half the territory it had conquered during the summer.

 Words to Know

Embargo: A government order that prohibits all commercial ship traffic from entering or leaving a harbor; Lord Loudoun placed an embargo on the entire Atlantic coast of America in 1756 in an attempt to stop illegal trading with the French.

Irregulars: Soldiers who were not part of the formal British Army, including troops and militia recruited in the American colonies; irregulars tended to have less military training and poorer equipment than British regulars.

Quakers: Members of the Society of Friends religious group, which originated in England in the seventeenth century and was brought to America by William Penn, founder of Pennsylvania Colony; among the Quakers' main principles was pacifism (a strong opposition to war and violence).

Regulars: Professional soldiers of the British Army; they tended to be highly trained and well equipped compared to irregulars from the American colonies.

Loudoun takes charge of British forces in North America

Meanwhile, the fighting continued in North America between the French and their Indian (Native American) allies and the British and their American colonists. British leaders in London were still upset about the defeat of General **Ed-**

People to Know

John Campbell, fourth earl of Loudoun (1705–1782): British general who served as commander-in-chief of British forces in North America, 1756–58.

Louis-Joseph, marquis de Montcalm-Gozon de Saint-Véran (1712–1759): French general who served as commander-in-chief of French forces in North America, 1756–59; led the capture of Forts Oswego and William Henry and died during the battle for Quebec.

Pierre François de Rigaud, marquis de Vaudreuil (1698–1778): Governor of New France from 1755 until the fall of Canada to the British in 1760.

ward Braddock (1695–1755; see entry) and the failure of their other military plans. They decided to replace William Shirley (1694–1771), who had become commander-in-chief upon Braddock's death, with an experienced military planner named John Campbell, fourth earl of Loudoun (1705–1782).

Like Braddock, Lord Loudoun held broad powers as commander-in-chief of all British and American armed forces in North America. But when he arrived in mid-1756, he found that Shirley had already planned several military campaigns for the year. For example, Shirley had ordered seven thousand colonial troops to gather at Fort Edward and Fort William Henry, British forts located on the Hudson River and Lake George in northern New York. These forces were to be used in an attack against Fort St. Frédéric, a French stronghold at Crown Point on Lake Champlain. Shirley had also put plans in place to capture French forts on Lake Ontario and the St. Lawrence River in order to cut off French supply routes to the west from Montreal.

Since most of the colonial troops were already in place, Loudoun decided to include the attack on Fort St. Frédéric in his plans. But Loudoun did not have much faith in "irregular" colonial troops (volunteers and recruits from the American colonies; they usually received less training than their British counterparts) and preferred to make the attack using "regular" (professional) British Army soldiers. Loudoun knew that there were three thousand highly trained British soldiers waiting for orders in Albany, so he decided to add them to the forces headed for Crown Point. Loudoun did not realize that Shirley had kept the British and colonial soldiers apart on purpose. British leaders in London had recently created new rules that made the colonial troops subject to the same strict discipline and harsh punishments as the regular troops. At the same time, however, colonial officers—regardless of their rank or level of experience—were expected to take orders from regular officers. These rules had made it difficult for Shirley to recruit an army from the colonies. To overcome resistance, he had promised the colonial forces that they would not have to serve alongside any regulars. This way, they would not have to worry about the new rules.

When Loudoun tried to combine the British and colonial forces for the attack on Fort St. Frédéric, the colonials threatened to quit and return to their homes. The commander-in-chief became furious about what he viewed as their unprofessional behavior. He could not believe that the American forces would not submit to British Army rules and discipline. But this incident was only the beginning of Loudoun's problems. He soon began using his powers as commander-in-chief to issue orders to the colonial governors. He expected them to provide money, men, and supplies for his armies, but they often stalled or simply refused his requests. Loudoun also expected the people of Albany and other cities to provide shelter for British soldiers. He thought the colonists should gladly offer quarters for the troops that had come to defend them. But most people refused to allow soldiers to stay in their homes unless the army paid for their room and board. These disputes convinced Loudoun that all Americans were ungrateful and did not understand the idea of serving a common cause.

The French military effort also received a new leader in mid-1756 when **Louis-Joseph, marquis de Montcalm-Gozon de Saint-Véran** (1712–1759; see entry), arrived in New France. An experienced general, Montcalm would lead the defense of French territory in North America for the next three years. New France also had a new governor general, Pierre François de Rigaud, marquis de Vaudreuil

William Shirley, British commander-in-chief following the death of Edward Braddock.
Reproduced by permission of The Granger Collection Ltd.

Marquis de Vaudreuil, Governor General of New France

Pierre François de Rigaud, marquis de Vaudreuil-Cavagnal, was born on November 22, 1698, in Quebec, the capital of the French colony of New France. His father, Philippe de Rigaud, marquis de Vaudreuil, was the governor general of New France at the time of his birth. The younger Vaudreuil joined the French Army at the age of six and achieved the rank of captain by the time he was a teenager. In 1733, he was appointed governor of the Canadian city of Trois-Rivières, and nine years later he became governor of the French colony of Louisiana.

By the time Vaudreuil returned to France in 1753, he was widely viewed as a capable colonial official. In 1755—just as the French and British began fighting for control of North America—he returned to Quebec as the governor general of New France. Having grown up in Canada, Vaudreuil was familiar with the North American wilderness and felt confident that he

knew what sort of warfare would succeed under those conditions. He began sending his Indian allies to conduct violent raids along the frontier of the British colonies. He believed that such raids would prevent British settlers from moving into disputed regions and allow the French to maintain control over the Ohio Country.

In 1756, the French government sent an experienced general, Louis-Joseph, marquis de Montcalm, to take charge of French military forces in North America. Vaudreuil and Montcalm immediately entered into a series of disagreements. As governor of New France, Vaudreuil thought that he should be responsible for the control of the war against the British. But as leader of the troops in the field, Montcalm felt that he should dictate the French military strategy.

One of the main sources of conflict between the two men concerned the use of Indian allies. Vaudreuil felt that Indian allies gave the French an important advantage

(1698–1778; see box), who had replaced Ange Duquesne de Menneville, marquis de Duquesne (1700–1778) in 1755. Vaudreuil was a strong believer in wilderness warfare. He wanted to use France's Indian allies to conduct raids along the western frontier of the British colonies. If the British had to worry about defending the frontier, Vaudreuil was convinced they would be less able to launch an invasion of Canada. But as a traditional European military leader, Montcalm was horrified by the style of warfare used by the Indians. He distrusted the Indians and was reluctant to use them in his military operations. He wanted to rely upon regular

Pierre François de Rigaud, marquis de Vaudreuil. *Courtesy of the Library of Congress.*

lable, Montcalm was reluctant to use them in his military campaigns. In the meantime, corrupt officials in Vaudreuil's government stole money and supplies that the French government sent to support the army. Montcalm suspected that Vaudreuil was involved in these illegal activities.

After Montcalm was killed in the Battle of Quebec in 1759, Vaudreuil collected the French forces and retreated to Montreal. The following year, three British armies converged on the city. Vaudreuil surrendered on September 8, 1760, to end the French and Indian War in North America. Afterward, he sailed to France with other officials from the colonial government. Vaudreuil was charged with corruption and other crimes relating to his service as governor general of New France, but he was found not guilty. Nevertheless, the accusations ended his career in government service. He retired to his estate, where he lived quietly until his death in 1778.

over the British. He noted that his strategy of conducting raids on British settlements had been successful during the previous year. But Montcalm favored a more traditional approach to warfare. Convinced that the Indians were uncivilized and uncontrol-

French Army troops and to conduct the war in a more civilized manner.

French capture Fort Oswego

As Lord Loudoun struggled to organize the British war effort, Montcalm and the French went on the offensive. Their first target was Fort Oswego, located on the southern shore of Lake Ontario at the mouth of the Oswego River (near the site of modern-day Syracuse, New York). The fort itself was situat-

Louis-Joseph, marquis de Montcalm-Gozon de Saint-Véran. *Reproduced by permission of Getty Images.*

ed on a low rise overlooking the lake. On each side of the fort were steep hills on which the British had built small outposts. Holding the fort for the British were 1,135 troops under the command of Lieutenant Colonel James Mercer.

On August 10, 1756, Montcalm brought a 3,000-man army to attack the fort. His forces consisted of 1,300 highly trained French soldiers, 1,500 Canadian militia, and 250 Indians from six different nations. The French started out by attacking the two high outposts and capturing them easily. Then they aimed their cannons down at the poorly constructed British fort. One of the cannonballs killed Mercer, and the fort surrendered a short time later. Montcalm's forces destroyed the fort and took all of the boats, cannons, guns, and other supplies they could find. Montcalm ordered that all the remaining British soldiers be taken as prisoners of war. He promised to protect the prisoners and transport them to Montreal for the duration of the war.

But Montcalm's Indian allies had other ideas. Unlike the French and Canadian forces, they were not paid to take part in the battle. They had joined the fight in order to demonstrate their courage. Their only payment came in the form of the trophies they collected—captives, scalps, weapons, and supplies. The Indians became angry when they heard about Montcalm's plan for the British prisoners. They ended up killing between thirty and one hundred British soldiers and taking many more captive. Montcalm was outraged by the Indians' behavior. In fact, he secretly paid ransom to reclaim some of the prisoners.

Following the French capture of Fort Oswego, Loudoun called off the planned attack against Crown Point. Instead, he ordered the colonial soldiers gathered at Fort William Henry to improve the fort and prepare to defend it against an attack by the French. By the end of the summer, the British forces stationed along the northern border of the colonies were there for defensive purposes only.

Loudoun plans attack of Louisbourg

Desperate to undertake some offensive action against the French, Loudoun began planning a huge military campaign for 1757. He decided to attack Louisbourg, an important port city on Cape Breton Island, along the Atlantic coast of New France. If the British captured Louisbourg, they could continue down the St. Lawrence River to attack Quebec and Montreal. Loudoun knew that his plan left the northern frontier of the colonies exposed to attacks by France, but he decided to move forward anyway.

Loudoun had spent the winter of 1756–57 improving the systems for collecting supplies and transporting them around the colonies. He also started recruiting colonial soldiers in small companies instead of large regiments so that he could mix them more easily with British Army units. Finally, Loudoun placed an embargo (a government order that prohibits commercial ships from entering or leaving a port) on the Atlantic coast in an attempt to stop illegal trading with the French in Canada and the West Indies. Only military ships were allowed to come and go in port cities from Maine to Georgia. At first, the colonies willingly obeyed Loudoun's order, believing that it would be a temporary war measure. As the embargo continued for months, however, it began to cause hardships for merchants and farmers who needed to send or receive goods from overseas markets. Over time, people in the colonies came to resent the commander-in-chief. They felt that he did not care about their welfare. Eventually, the colonial governors forced Loudoun to reopen the ports by refusing to supply his army.

Loudoun set sail for Louisbourg from New York on June 20. He took along a force of six thousand men on one hundred ships, making it the largest expeditionary force ever to set sail from an American port. Loudoun's forces arrived in Halifax, Nova Scotia, ten days later. They waited there another ten days until a Royal Navy squadron (group of ships) came to escort them. Before the attack could begin, however, the Royal Navy

British general Lord Loudoun. *Reproduced by permission of The Granger Collection Ltd.*

wanted to find out how many French Navy ships they would face in Louisbourg. Finally, on August 4, a scout ship returned to report that the French had a huge fleet of three squadrons in Louisbourg. Since it was too late in the summer to bring more Royal Navy squadrons to the area, Loudoun decided that there was no way his mission would succeed. He reluctantly called off the attack and ordered all the ships to return to New York.

French destroy Fort William Henry

Around the same time as Loudoun left for Louisbourg, he sent fifty–five hundred colonial troops and two regiments of British Army regulars under General Daniel Webb to defend the northern frontier in New York. One of the main British strongholds in this region, Fort William Henry, located at the south end of Lake George, had been damaged by a surprise attack in mid-March. A force of fifteen hundred French, Canadians, and Indians under François-Pierre Rigaud had destroyed several outbuildings as well as some boats and supplies. Although the British had turned back the attack, it had left the fort vulnerable to further attacks via water.

As it turned out, the French were planning a major offensive against Fort William Henry. The series of French military successes over the previous two years—including the defeat of Braddock and the capture of Fort Oswego—had attracted the attention of many Indian nations. The French were able to recruit two thousand warriors from thirty-three different nations to take part in the attack of Fort William

Henry. Montcalm brought the Indians, along with six thousand French regulars and Canadian militia, to Fort Carillon at the north end of Lake George.

Defending Fort William Henry were fifteen hundred men under the command of Lieutenant Colonel George Monro (c. 1700–1757), an aging officer who had never served in the field before. In late July, Monro heard a rumor that eight thousand enemy forces had gathered across the lake from his position. He sent five companies of colonial troops across the lake by boat to check out the rumor, but the British boats were ambushed by five hundred Indians and Canadians. Only four of the twenty-two British boats escaped the trap, and three-quarters of the men were killed or captured. General Webb was making his first visit to Fort William Henry when the survivors straggled back to safety. He retreated to Fort Edward and sent back one thousand reinforcements to help Monro hold the fort.

On the morning of August 3, the British and colonial defenders saw 150 Indian war canoes and 250 French bateaux (small, flat-bottomed boats) coming toward them across the lake. The boats carried sixty-five hundred men and some artillery. Monro knew that Fort William Henry could not withstand artillery fire for very long. He needed troops from Fort Edward to attack Montcalm's forces before they finished setting up the artillery. But Webb refused to send any more troops, deciding that he needed them to defend Fort Edward.

Over the next few days, Fort William Henry was battered by enemy shells. The French used European siege tactics, which involved moving their guns ever closer to the fort. On August 9, Monro was forced to surrender the fort. In his efforts to conduct the war in a civilized manner, Montcalm negotiated honorable terms of surrender with the British forces. He allowed the men to keep their personal possessions and march to Fort Edward, as long as they promised not to fight against the French anymore. Once again, however, Montcalm had failed to consider his Indian allies when making the deal.

Angry at being left out of the settlement, the Indians became determined to take the trophies they felt they had earned. What followed has been called "the massacre of Fort William Henry." As the British forces gathered their wounded

America's Western Frontier Comes Under Attack

By 1756, most of the Indian nations around the Great Lakes and in the Ohio Country had thrown their support behind the French. Some had tried to form an alliance with the British, but British leaders had not been interested. In some cases, the British had offended the Indians and turned them into enemies. In other cases, the French had brought the Indians to their side by negotiating with them and offering gifts.

The alliance between the French and the Indians created a dangerous situation along the western frontier of the American colonies. French leaders encouraged the Indians to conduct raids on British settlements stretching across hundreds of miles in western Pennsylvania, Maryland, and Virginia. In these raids, the Indians often killed the British settlers or took them as prisoners. They also stole their belongings and burned down their homesteads. The Indians viewed the raids as a way to get rid of the British and reclaim their land. Indian warriors also earned the respect of their people by demonstrating their bravery in battle. Returning from a raid with trophies—such as live prisoners, the scalps of people they had killed, or valuable items taken from homes or forts—was a way for the warriors to prove their courage.

The constant raids caused the British settlers to live in fear. Many were forced to abandon their homesteads and return to the cities. Others wrote letters to colonial leaders, begging for help in defending themselves. "We are in as bad circumstances as ever any poor Christians were ever in, for the cries of widowers, widows, fatherless and motherless children are enough to pierce the most hardest of hearts," a settler named Adam Hoops wrote to Governor Robert Hunter Morris (1700–1764) of Pennsylvania. "Likewise it's a very sorrowful [sad] spectacle to see those that escaped with their lives with not a mouthful to eat, or bed to lie on, or clothes to cover their nakedness, or keep them warm, but all they had consumed into ashes."

For the most part, the American colonies were not able to protect their frontiers from the Indian raids. The colonies built a weak chain of forts along the western edge of their territories. Only a few of these forts were large and strong enough to serve as a base for soldiers. The others mainly provided traders and settlers with a safer place to stay during raids. The most important of these forts were Fort Augusta on the Susquehanna River in Pennsylvania, Forts Cumberland and Frederick in Maryland, and Fort Loudoun in Virginia.

and began marching toward Fort Edward, they were brutally attacked by the Indians. Up to 185 men were killed and between 300 and 500 were taken prisoner. Montcalm was horri-

An illustration of an Indian attack. *Reproduced by permission of the Corbis Corporation.*

Maryland spent very little money or effort defending its relatively small frontier. By the fall of 1756, colonial leaders decided that they could no longer defend Fort Cumberland and abandoned it. Virginia sent a regiment of colonial soldiers under the command of **George Washington** (1732–1799; see entry) to patrol its frontier. But Washington's forces included only between four hundred and seven hundred men, and they were expected to protect 18 forts and 350 miles of frontier. To make the job even tougher, Washington's men received very little pay and often faced supply shortages.

Settlers along the Pennsylvania frontier probably suffered the most from Indian raids. Hundreds of settlers were killed in 1756, when Indian raids swept within seventy miles of Philadelphia. Yet colonial leaders refused to spend money or send troops to defend the frontier. Pennsylvania's assembly was controlled by members of the Quaker religion. One of the guiding principles of Quakerism is pacifism, which prohibits the support of violence or war in any form, regardless of circumstances. Eventually, however, public outcry about the situation on the frontier forced the Quakers to leave public office.

At this point, the Quakers began trying to negotiate a peaceful settlement with the Delaware Indians—the largest Indian nation in the area. The Quakers discovered that the raids had created hardships for the Indians as well as for the settlers. Taking part in raids had kept the Delaware men from their usual jobs of hunting and harvesting crops. As a result, the Delaware people faced severe shortages of food and other supplies. By 1757, the Quakers had made some progress in their negotiations, and it looked as if the Delawares might agree to stop the raids in exchange for the return of tribal lands and gifts of trade goods.

fied at this turn of events. He tried to use his French troops to force the Indians to give up their captives, but the Indians responded by killing the prisoners so that they would have a scalp as a trophy. Once they were satisfied with the trophies they had collected, the Indians slipped into the woods and headed for home.

Over the following days and weeks, Montcalm continued trying to retrieve the British prisoners by paying ransom to the Indians. He knew that his honor was at stake, since he had failed to live up to his end of the surrender agreement. He also worried that the incident would make British leaders less willing to negotiate if they captured French forts in the future. About two hundred prisoners were recovered through Montcalm's efforts, as well as those of Vaudreuil in Montreal. In the meantime, British survivors trickled into Fort Edward for a week after the battle. Their stories created strong feelings against the French and the Indians among British leaders and the American colonists.

The incident at Fort William Henry turned out badly for the Indians as well. The British forces defending the fort had been suffering from smallpox (a disease caused by a virus), which the warriors carried back to their people. It created a terrible epidemic among the western tribes that caused a great deal of suffering and death. Between the smallpox epidemic and Montcalm's actions in negotiating a surrender—which the Indians viewed as a breach of trust—the Indians never turned out in support of the French in such great numbers again.

Following his victory, Montcalm destroyed Fort William Henry and returned to Fort Carillon. He chose not to attack Fort Edward, located a short distance to the south along the Hudson River. After all, most of the Indians had already left, and many of his Canadian troops needed to return home to harvest their crops. Still, the capture of Fort William Henry left the British in a vulnerable position. Only little Fort Edward stood between the French and several important targets, including the trading center of Albany and New York City itself.

1758: The British Turn the Tide

6

As 1758 began, the French and Indian War (1754–63; known in Europe as the Seven Years' War) had caused three years of frustration and disappointment for the British. The French had launched successful offensive attacks and taken control of two important British forts: Fort Oswego on Lake Ontario and Fort William Henry on Lake George. In addition, Indian (Native American) raids had created suffering and hardship for settlers along the western frontier of the American colonies. Meanwhile, British forces had failed in their attempts to capture Fort Duquesne at the Forks of the Ohio River, Fort St. Frédéric on Lake Champlain, and the port city of Louisbourg on Cape Breton Island.

One major factor in the collapse of the British war effort was the lack of cooperation between John Campbell, fourth earl of Loudoun (1705–1782), the commander-in-chief of British forces in North America, and the leaders of the American colonies. Loudoun had terrible problems dealing with the colonists throughout his two years as commander-in-chief. Colonial leaders always resisted giving him the money, supplies, and manpower he demanded. Loudoun al-

Words to Know

Ohio Country: A vast wilderness that stretched from the Great Lakes in the north to the Ohio River in the South, and from the Allegheny Mountains in the east to the Mississippi River in the west; the French and British fought for control of this region, which lay between the French and British colonies in North America.

Siege: A military strategy that involves surrounding a target, cutting it off from outside help and supplies, and using artillery to break down its defenses.

ways responded by threatening to use force to get what he wanted. He never tried to compromise or work together with the colonies to achieve his goals. Over time, the colonists came to view Loudoun as a threat to their rights and freedom, and they grew determined to resist him in any way possible.

The problems between Loudoun and the Americans reached a peak in early 1758. Many colonists thought that they should have the same rights as British citizens. They also believed the colonial governments should not have to answer to a military leader. Men in New England not only refused to volunteer to serve in Loudoun's army, they also began holding violent protests against army recruiting. In February, colonial leaders held a meeting to decide amongst themselves how many troops to provide for Loudoun's upcoming military campaigns. They thought Loudoun's demands were unreasonable and did not take local conditions and laws into account. But as commander-in-chief, Loudoun felt he should decide how many men each colony should provide. He saw this meeting as a direct challenge to his authority. As this struggle continued into March, Loudoun received word from Great Britain that he had been removed from command.

Pitt takes over the British war effort

Major General James Abercromby (1706–1781), who had served as Loudoun's second-in-command, became the top British officer in North America. (His last name was sometimes spelled Abercrombie.) But the man in charge of the war effort was **William Pitt** (1708–1788; see entry), an ambitious and influential politician who had become secretary of state in the British government. Before this time, most British leaders had felt that the war in North America was less important than the war in Europe. But Pitt recognized that England was too small to become a dominant power in Europe on its own.

He decided that the key to defeating the French was to build a vast British empire that stretched around the world. If England controlled colonies that produced sugar, timber, cotton, grains, metals, and other goods that people needed, then it would be a very powerful nation.

Based on this new idea, Pitt decided to avoid using British troops in Europe, where France was strongest. Instead, he provided a great sum of money to help his European allies build up their armies to fight France. Pitt's main strategy for defeating France involved attacking its colonies around the world. He planned to send thousands of British troops to North America and launch an invasion of Canada. An important part of this plan involved using the powerful British Navy to control shipping across the Atlantic Ocean. This measure would prevent France from supplying its colonies from overseas. Another part of Pitt's plan involved gaining the support of the American colonists for the war effort. He did this by reversing many of the policies that had caused problems for Loudoun. Instead of ordering the colonies around and forcing them to provide money and troops, Pitt began treating them like allies and asking for their help. He offered money to the colonial governments in exchange for their aid in the invasion of New France. He also made sure that colonial officers in the army held the same status as British officers of the same rank.

People across the American colonies greeted Pitt's new policies with a burst of patriotic enthusiasm.

People to Know

James Abercromby (1706–1781): British general who served as commander-in-chief of British forces in North America in 1758 and suffered a terrible defeat in the Battle of Ticonderoga.

Jeffery Amherst (1717–1797): British military leader who became commander-in-chief of British forces in North America in 1758 and led the siege of Louisbourg and capture of Montreal.

John Bradstreet (c. 1711–1774): British military leader who captured Fort Frontenac and ended French control of Lake Ontario.

John Forbes (1710–1759): British military leader who captured Fort Duquesne in 1758 and established Fort Pitt on the site.

John Campbell, fourth earl of Loudoun (1705–1782): British general who served as commander-in-chief of British forces in North America, 1756–58.

Louis-Joseph, marquis de Montcalm-Gozon de Saint-Véran (1712–1759): French general who served as commander-in-chief of French forces in North America, 1756–59; led the capture of Forts Oswego and William Henry and died during the battle for Quebec.

William Pitt (1708–1788): British political leader who took control of the North American war effort in 1757; his policies gained the support of the American colonists.

British politician William Pitt, who took control of the North American war effort in 1757 and gained the support of American colonists. *Reproduced by permission of Getty Images.*

Massachusetts Colony, for example, had refused to give Loudoun twenty-one hundred troops. But after Pitt changed the policies, the colony voted to provide seven thousand troops. Altogether, the American colonies agreed to provide twenty-three thousand soldiers to help force the French out of North America. Unlike before, when the colonial troops consisted mostly of men from the lower classes who were forced to serve, these troops were made up mostly of volunteers who came from higher social classes and education levels.

Pitt came up with a three-part plan for the invasion of Canada. The first part of the plan involved capturing the fortified (strengthened and secured by forts) port city of Louisbourg (located on the Atlantic coast, north of Maine), which Loudoun had failed to accomplish in 1757. Louisbourg guarded the entrance to the St. Lawrence River, which was the main water route to the major Canadian cities of Quebec and Montreal. The second part of Pitt's plan involved capturing Fort Carillon (known as Ticonderoga by the British) at the north end of Lake George. This French stronghold blocked a possible invasion route up Lake Champlain into Canada. The third part of Pitt's plan involved capturing Fort Duquesne in the Ohio Country. This French fort served as a supply base for the Indian raids that plagued the western frontier of the American colonies.

These three military operations would involve the largest forces that had ever fought in North America. The Louisbourg expedition, under Major General **Jeffery Amherst** (1717–1797; see entry), would include fourteen thousand troops. General Abercromby would use twenty-five thousand men to attack Fort Carillon and defend the northern border of New York. The attack on Fort Duquesne, led by Major General **John Forbes** (1710–1759; see entry), would involve seven thousand soldiers. The total forces were about equally split between regular British Army soldiers and irregular colonial troops.

Problems in New France

As the British were preparing for an all-out invasion of Canada, the French were suffering a series of setbacks in their North American war effort, due in large part to the fact that the French military and political leaders in the colony of New France did not get along. **Louis-Joseph, marquis de Montcalm-Gozon de Saint-Véran** (1712–1759; see entry), was the commander of French and Canadian armed forces. Pierre François de Rigaud, marquis de Vaudreuil (1698–1778; see box in chapter 5), was the governor general of New France. The two men disagreed over the use of Indian allies, strategies for conducting the war, and who should get credit for victories. In addition, Montcalm was disgusted by the corruption he saw in the government of New France. He believed that Vaudreuil and his cabinet stole money and supplies from France that should have gone to the army.

Montcalm needed all the help he could get from France because the French Canadian population was simply too small to provide enough food, supplies, and soldiers to defend Canada against the British. The British population in North America was ten times larger than the French population. In fact, the fifty thousand troops that Pitt planned to use in his invasion of Canada was equal to about two-thirds of the entire population of New France. Montcalm commanded only about twenty-five thousand total troops, including French regulars and Canadian militia. Most of the Indians who had supported the French in the early years of the war were no longer actively involved.

In addition, Canada was experiencing extreme food shortages during this time. These shortages occurred due to a series of poor harvests and the increasing success of the British Navy in preventing supplies from reaching the colony from France. Food shortages affected not only the army, but also people in the cities of New France. Finally, the French government had its hands full fighting the war in Europe. This situation prevented the French from throwing their full support behind Montcalm's forces in North America.

British general James Abercromby, who suffered a terrible defeat at the Battle of Ticonderoga. *Reproduced by permission of Getty Images.*

Abercromby loses the Battle of Ticonderoga

Despite the problems facing New France, Montcalm managed to hand the British another embarrassing defeat in mid-1758. After stationing some of his forces along New York's northern border, Abercromby moved fifteen thousand troops into position for the attack on Fort Carillon in early July. The attack itself would be led by a field general, Lord George Augustus Howe (1724–1758). Howe was an excellent soldier who was trained in wilderness warfare, and his troops respected him for his fairness and bravery. Howe gathered his forces—which included nine thousand colonial troops and six thousand British soldiers—at the ruins of Fort William Henry. They made their way north across Lake George in one thousand small boats and landed on the northwestern shore on July 6. Howe planned to march through the woods and approach Fort Carillon from the rear.

As some of the men set up camp, Howe led a small party forward to gather information about the French forces. They ended up running into a group of 350 French soldiers and exchanging gunfire. Howe was shot in the chest and killed. Abercromby took over command of the remaining forces, but the inexperienced general had trouble deciding what to do. He wasted several days sending out scouts and changing plans, and his lack of leadership caused the army to lose the order and discipline it had shown under Howe. In addition, the delay in the British offensive gave French forces time to prepare for the attack.

When Abercromby finally moved forward, he attacked the fort exactly where Montcalm expected him to. The French had used the extra time to build a huge wall of logs on a ridge behind the fort. They placed shooting platforms along the top of the wall. Then they created a barrier called an abatis on the slope leading up to the wall. The abatis was made by cutting down hundreds of trees and letting them fall so that the treetops formed a tangled mess facing the enemy forces. The troops then sharpened the branches so that they formed a barrier as effective as rolls of barbed wire.

Although Abercromby was aware of these defenses, he chose to make his attack from this direction anyway. He sent wave after wave of British soldiers toward the fort, where they either became tangled in the abatis or were shot by the French. A few British soldiers made it through the defenses and scaled the wall, only to be stabbed by the sharp bayonets attached to the French guns. Even though the French forces were outnumbered fifteen thousand to four thousand, they managed to hold off seven British charges. By the time Abercromby finally ordered a retreat, two thousand of his men were dead or wounded.

The defeat at Ticonderoga (see box) was terribly humiliating for the British. In fact, it was probably the second-worst incident of the war, after the defeat of British commander-in-chief **Edward Braddock** (1695–1755; see entry) on the Monongahela River in 1755. Abercromby's forces bitterly criticized the general for his shameful performance, calling him "Mrs. Nanny Cromby" or "Granny." Historians also place the blame for the defeat on Abercromby for attempting to storm a well-defended position instead of choosing another option. For example, Abercromby could have brought his cannons and artillery forward and battered the French defenses. He also could have sent troops up nearby Mount Defiance, which towered above the fort, and sent artillery fire down into it. Finally, he could have forced the fort to surrender by cutting off the supply road to Fort St. Frédéric on Lake Champlain. Instead, he was defeated by an army only a fraction of the size of his own.

Amherst captures Louisbourg

As it turned out, however, Abercromby's defeat in the Battle of Ticonderoga was the only dark spot for the British war effort in North America in 1758. The British came back with three important victories to turn the tide of the war in

British ships surround the walled city of Louisbourg during the siege of 1758. In the foreground at Lighthouse Point, soldiers direct the building of fortifications. *Engraving by P. Canot. Reproduced by permission of Getty Images.*

their favor. Around the same time that Abercromby was moving his forces into place for the attack on Fort Carillon, Major General Jeffery Amherst was transporting twelve thousand troops (mostly regular British Army) up the Atlantic coast by ship for an attack on Louisbourg. Defending the city were thirty-two hundred regular French Army soldiers and some armed residents under Augustin de Drucour (1703–1762), the governor of Louisbourg. In addition, Louisbourg's sheltered harbor was full of French warships.

Amherst planned to lay siege to Louisbourg. A siege is a military strategy that involves surrounding a target, cutting it off from outside help and supplies, and using artillery to break down its defenses. The first British forces landed on June 8, and a month later they had surrounded Louisbourg and begun pounding it with artillery fire. "There is not a house in the place that has not felt the effects of this formidable [strong] artillery," a French officer wrote in his diary. "From yesterday morning till seven o'clock this evening we reckon

A British Soldier Describes the Battle of Ticonderoga

The Battle of Ticonderoga was a terrible defeat for the British. General James Abercromby sent wave after wave of soldiers to attack Fort Carillon, a French stronghold that was protected by a large log wall. Most of these soldiers were killed or wounded by the French defenders of the fort. Even though the British outnumbered the French fifteen thousand to four thousand, the attack failed and left two thousand British soldiers dead or wounded. In the following excerpt from a war memoir, a British soldier remembers the scene of the battle:

Our orders were to [run] to the breast work [wall] and get in if we could. But their lines were full, and they killed our men so fast, that we could not gain it. We got behind trees, logs and stumps, and covered ourselves as we could from the enemy's fire. The ground was strewed with the dead and dying. It happened that I got behind a white-oak stump, which was so small that I had to lay on my side, and stretch myself; the [musket] balls striking the ground within a hand's breadth of me every moment, and I could hear the men screaming, and see them dying all around me. I lay there some time. A man could not stand erect without being hit, any more than he could stand out in a shower, without having drops of rain fall upon him; for the balls came by handsfull. It was a clear day—a little air stirring. Once in a while the enemy would cease firing a minute or two, to have the smoke clear away, so that they might take better aim.

Fighting during the Battle of Ticonderoga.
Reproduced by permission of the Corbis Corporation.

In one of these intervals I sprang from my perilous [dangerous] situation, and gained a stand [position] which I thought would be more secure, behind a large pine log, where several of my comrades had already taken shelter but the balls came here as thick as ever. One of the men raised his head a little above the log, and a ball struck him in the centre of the forehead.... We lay there till near sunset and, not receiving orders from any officer, the men crept off, leaving all the dead, and most of the wounded.

Source: Perry, David. Recollections of an Old Soldier ... Written by Himself. *Windsor, VT: 1822 (later published in* Magazine of History *137, 1928).*

that a thousand or twelve hundred bombs, great and small, have been thrown into the town, accompanied all the time by the fire of forty pieces of cannon, served with an activity not often seen." The British finally broke through Louisbourg's defenses and forced the city to surrender on July 26.

Bradstreet captures Fort Frontenac

A few days after Abercromby's defeat at Ticonderoga, one of his young officers, Lieutenant Colonel John Bradstreet (c. 1711–1774), convinced the general to add a fourth part to the British Army's plan for the year. Bradstreet wanted to lead an attack on Fort Frontenac, an important French trading base located at the east end of Lake Ontario. The fort provided supplies to Fort Duquesne and other western forts, as well as to the Indians of the Ohio Country. It also served as a base for the French warships that patrolled Lake Ontario. Finally, the fort provided a vital communications link between Quebec and French settlements to the west.

In August, Bradstreet began moving up the Mohawk River with about five thousand of Abercromby's troops. To keep the French from learning about the mission, Bradstreet pretended that they were going to rebuild Fort Bull, a British fort that had been located at the Great Carrying Place—a spot where Indians carried their canoes between the Mohawk and Onondaga Rivers. He only revealed the true mission once the troops had arrived at the Great Carrying Place. Then his men continued across Lake Ontario by boat and landed near the French stronghold. Bradstreet was surprised that the fort offered very little resistance as his men moved their cannons into position for an assault on August 27. The French surrendered a few hours after the British began firing on the fort.

As it turned out, Fort Frontenac contained only about one hundred French troops, plus some women and children. The rest of the French forces had gone to help defend Fort Carillon against Abercromby's attack. But the fort was stuffed with valuable trade goods—including furs, food, clothing, weapons, and ammunition—that were intended to supply Fort Duquesne and the western Indians. Bradstreet and his men collected everything they could carry and destroyed the rest. They also took control of the French ships that had patrolled Lake Ontario. They allowed the French soldiers and their families to return to Montreal, with the agreement that they would arrange for the release of an equal number of

British prisoners of war. When Bradstreet returned from his successful mission, the ambitious young officer tried to convince Abercromby to push their advantage and attack the French forts at Niagara and Detroit. But the old general refused and allowed his troops to go home for the winter. In September, Pitt removed Abercromby from command and named Amherst the top British officer in North America.

French surrender Fort Duquesne

The third part of Pitt's plan—the expedition to attack Fort Duquesne—also got underway during the summer of 1758. The forces consisted of fifteen hundred British regulars and forty-eight hundred colonial troops under Major General John Forbes. Forbes was a brilliant officer cursed

British major general John Forbes. *Courtesy of the Library of Congress.*

with terrible health. He suffered from a painful skin condition that made it difficult for him to move, and he also caught a serious intestinal illness called dysentery. As a result, the only way for him to advance with his troops was by riding in a hammock strung between two horses. One of the officers accompanying Forbes was **George Washington** (1732–1799; see entry), who had first visited the Forks of the Ohio during his diplomatic mission in 1753.

Forbes and his army made their way slowly through Pennsylvania toward Fort Duquesne, building a road and a series of defensive outposts along the way. On September 14, an advance party of eight hundred men led by Major James Grant (1720–1806) came within a mile of the French fort. French soldiers and Indian warriors came pouring out of the fort and attacked Grant's forces. Washington's Virginia regiment fought bravely and allowed the remaining British troops to retreat. Still, three hundred men were killed, wounded, or captured in the battle.

The Indians who had taken part in the attack collected their trophies and went home, leaving only three hundred French soldiers to defend Fort Duquesne. Forbes was about to abandon his mission when he learned that Bradstreet had captured Fort Frontenac and destroyed the supplies that were headed for Fort Duquesne. Figuring that the French must be running low on supplies, Forbes decided to wait and prepare for another attack. In November, he ordered a full-scale attack on Fort Duquesne. As his men approached the fort, however, they heard a series of explosions. The French had realized that they could not defend the fort against the British attack. They decided to destroy it rather than allow it to fall into enemy hands.

The British built a new fort at the Forks of the Ohio and called it Fort Pitt. The success of Forbes's mission cut the connection between the French colonies along the Mississippi River and those in Canada and claimed the Ohio Country for Great Britain. Forbes returned to Philadelphia, where he died a few months later. Around this same time, Washington ended his involvement in the war. Convinced that the destruction of Fort Duquesne would bring peace to the Virginia frontier, Washington resigned from the Virginia militia and returned to his estate to begin a political career.

War continues in Europe and around the world

Pitt and other British leaders were pleased to hear about the victories over the French in North America. But they soon had to focus their attention on the war in Europe. Great Britain's ally, King Frederick (1712–1786) of Prussia, had been fighting against Russia and Austria and appeared weak. Pitt had been reluctant to send British troops to help Frederick. But he eventually agreed to send enough men to hold the port of Emden on the North Sea, which Prince Ferdinand (1721–1792) of Brunswick (King Frederick's brother-in-law) had captured from the French.

The British added several more victories around the world to their total for 1758. They took control of a series of French trading posts along the west coast of Africa. They also attacked the island of Martinique in the Caribbean, which was valuable to France because of its sugar exports. Pitt hoped that he would be able to exchange Martinique for the captured British military base on the Mediterranean island of Minorca if the French and British eventually tried to negotiate peace.

1759: The Fall of Canada

The military successes of 1758 in the French and Indian War (1754–63; known in Europe as the Seven Years' War) put the British in a strong position to launch an invasion of Canada the following year. British troops had captured Louisbourg, the fortified city that guarded the entrance to the St. Lawrence River. This victory would allow British ships to sail up the river to attack the major Canadian cities of Quebec and Montreal. The British had also taken control of Lake Ontario and cut off communications between the eastern and western sections of New France. **William Pitt** (1708–1788; see entry), the British secretary of state, decided that the time had come to invade Canada. In 1759, he came up with a three-part plan to achieve this goal.

The first part of Pitt's plan involved attacking Fort Niagara on Lake Ontario, which stood between the British and several French forts to the west. In the second part of Pitt's plan, British and American forces under General **Jeffery Amherst** (1717–1797; see entry) would attack Fort Carillon at Ticonderoga on Lake Champlain. The successful capture of this French stronghold would allow British forces to continue northward across the lake toward Montreal. Finally, the third part of Pitt's plan called for British forces under General **James Wolfe** (1727–1759; see entry) to move up the St. Lawrence from Louisbourg and attack Quebec, the capital of New France.

In preparation for the invasion of Canada, Pitt wrote to the governors of the American colonies asking for twenty thousand troops—the same level of support he had requested in 1758. By this time, the war had created shortages of money and men in the colonies. The governors had to pay high bounties (fees) to convince young men to serve in the army, but they finally managed to recruit seventeen thousand troops. Their efforts showed that they respected Pitt and felt like partners in his plans.

British take Fort Niagara and control the West

As part of their successful campaigns of 1758, the British had captured Fort Duquesne. Holding this French fort, located at the strategic point known as the Forks of the Ohio River (site of modern-day Pittsburgh), was key to the British gaining control of the Ohio Country. Once they seized the fort, the British immediately began building a huge new stronghold on the site. This new fort, which they called Fort Pitt, was ten times larger than Fort Duquesne. They planned to turn the fort into a center of trade in order to keep the Ohio Indians (Native Americans) on their side. In the meantime, French forces under Captain François-Marie le Marchand de Lignery (1703–1759) remained at Venango, a French stronghold on the Allegheny River north of the Forks. Lignery spent the winter of 1759 trying to convince the Indians to help him reclaim the Forks and reestablish French control of the Ohio Country.

 Words to Know

Iroquois Confederacy (Six Nations of the Iroquois): A powerful alliance of six Indian nations (the Cayuga, Mohawk, Oneida, Onondaga, Seneca, and Tuscarora) from the Iroquois language family.

Ohio Country: A vast wilderness that stretched from the Great Lakes in the north to the Ohio River in the south, and from the Allegheny Mountains in the east to the Mississippi River in the west; the French and British fought for control of this region, which lay between the French and British colonies in North America.

Siege: A military strategy that involves surrounding a target, cutting it off from outside help and supplies, and using artillery to break down its defenses.

People to Know

Jeffery Amherst (1717–1797): British military leader who became commander-in-chief of British forces in North America in 1758 and led the siege of Louisbourg and capture of Montreal.

Louis-Antoine de Bougainville (1729–1811): French military leader who served in the defense of Ticonderoga and Quebec; later became the first Frenchman to sail around the world; made several important contributions to science and geography.

William Johnson (1715–1774): British general who served as chief of Indian affairs and won the Battle of Lake George.

Louis-Joseph, marquis de Montcalm-Gozon de Saint-Véran (1712–1759): French general who served as commander-in-chief of French forces in North America, 1756–59; led the capture of Forts Oswego and William Henry and died during the battle for Quebec.

William Pitt (1708–1788): British political leader who took control of the North American war effort in 1757; his policies gained the support of the American colonists.

James Wolfe (1727–1759): British military leader who captured Louisbourg and was killed during the successful battle for Quebec.

But the continued British military success in 1759 ensured that Fort Pitt and the Ohio Country would remain the property of the king of England. As spring arrived, British and American forces under Brigadier General John Prideaux (1718–1759) launched an expedition to capture Fort Niagara. By mid-June, they had reached Oswego, a site on the southwestern shore of Lake Ontario that had held a British fort until it was destroyed by the French in 1756. Here they were met by **William Johnson** (1715–1774; see entry)—a British general and the king's official Indian representative—and one thousand Iroquois warriors. The Iroquois Confederacy had decided to provide direct support to the British in order to maintain their influence over the tribes of the Ohio Country. Prideaux left one thousand of his own troops at Oswego to begin rebuilding the fort. Then he continued across Lake Ontario toward Fort Niagara with Johnson and the Iroquois.

Prideaux's forces reached the fort on July 6. The commander of the French stronghold was Captain Pierre Pouchot (1712–1767). Confident that the Ohio Indians would warn him if the British came near, Pouchot had sent twenty-five hundred of his three thousand troops to Venango to help Lignery recapture the Forks. The French captain and his five hundred remaining troops were shocked when the British and Iroquois appeared and began preparing for a siege of the fort. In a siege, attacking forces surround their target and pound it with artillery fire until the defenses are weak enough for a full assault. The British spent several days digging protective trenches and then began shelling Fort Niagara on July 16. Prideaux was killed in the early days of the siege, forcing Johnson to take command of the British troops.

Pouchot was determined to hold the fort until reinforcements arrived from Venango. But the British knew that Lignery would bring his forces north to help defend Niagara. They built a log wall and an abatis (a defensive barrier that consists of felled trees with sharpened branches) to block the road to the fort. Lignery arrived on July 23 with a force of six hundred French soldiers and one thousand Indian allies. Before the battle began, the Indians on both sides held a conference and decided not to take part. Lignery's remaining force of six hundred French soldiers charged the British position in an attempt to break through to the fort. More than half of these men were killed or taken prisoner, and the others were forced to retreat. Pouchot surrendered Fort Niagara to Johnson two days later.

William Johnson, the British representative to the Indians. *Reproduced by permission of Getty Images.*

The capture of Fort Niagara gave the British control over the Ohio Country and much of the former French territory to the west. Without access to the road leading past Niagara Falls from Lake Ontario to Lake Erie, the French could not get supplies through to their western forts. They had no choice but to abandon Fort Toronto on Lake Ontario, Fort Presque Isle on Lake Erie, and Forts Le Boeuf and Machault (Venango) in the Ohio Country. The French maintained a few settlements in Illinois, and a few forts and trading posts in the upper Great Lakes, but these outposts could no longer communicate with the government of New France in Quebec.

Johnson, meanwhile, decided that the capture of Fort Niagara would be his last campaign. He resigned from the military to concentrate on his duties as the king's Indian representative. With Johnson gone, the British commander-in-

British general James Wolfe, who defeated the French in Quebec. *Reproduced by permission of Getty Images.*

chief, General Jeffery Amherst, sent Major General Thomas Gage (1719–1787) to take charge of the western posts.

Amherst captures Ticonderoga and Crown Point

The second part of Pitt's plan took shape at the same time as the siege of Fort Niagara. After spending months preparing for the attack, Amherst reached Fort Carillon at Ticonderoga on the south end of Lake Champlain on July 21. His ten thousand troops approached the fort in boats. Upon landing, they began digging trenches for a siege. But Amherst did not realize that the French had already abandoned the fort, leaving only a few soldiers to defend it. These soldiers destroyed Fort Carillon a few days after Amherst's arrival. The capture of the French stronghold cost Amherst the lives of five men and wounded thirty-one more. The outcome for the British was much better than a year earlier, when General James Abercromby (1706–1781) had suffered two thousand casualties (killed or wounded soldiers) in his failed attack on the fort.

After capturing Fort Carillon, Amherst moved his forces northward to Fort St. Frédéric at Crown Point on Lake Champlain. By the time the British forces arrived, however, the French had abandoned and destroyed that fort as well. This left only a couple of small and insignificant forts between Amherst and his ultimate target, the city of Montreal. But Amherst moved slowly and cautiously toward Montreal because he had not yet heard any news about the third part of Pitt's plan—Major General James Wolfe's attack on Quebec. If Wolfe had been defeated, then the French could transfer all of their forces to defend Montreal. By the time Amherst finally received a report on Wolfe's progress in mid-October, the approach of winter forced him to call off his expedition.

Wolfe and Montcalm battle for Quebec

Wolfe, a bold young officer who had taken part in the capture of Louisbourg in 1758, was thrilled to be asked to lead the attack on Quebec. In addition to twelve thousand British and American troops, Wolfe's expedition included a fleet of one hundred fifty ships and eighteen thousand sailors from the British Navy. Some of these ships were sent ahead to Louisbourg to prevent the French from sending supplies and additional troops to Quebec via the St. Lawrence. Although the British Navy managed to turn back or capture some French ships, a few still managed to sneak through the blockade. One of these ships carried **Louis-Antoine de Bougainville** (1729–1811; see entry), the top aide to French commander **Louis-Joseph, marquis de Montcalm-Gozon de Saint-Véran** (1712–1759; see entry). Bougainville brought Montcalm a document that French soldiers had captured. The document, which had belonged to General Amherst, outlined the British plans for the 1759 invasion of Canada.

British general Jeffery Amherst. *Courtesy of the Library of Congress.*

After looking over the British plans, Montcalm decided to focus on defending Quebec. The city sat atop high cliffs overlooking the St. Lawrence River and was surrounded by a wall that held many cannons. Montcalm felt confident that the guns along the cliffs would prevent the British from moving their ships past the city in order to cut off the French supply line from Montreal. He left two thousand soldiers within the walls of Quebec and arranged his remaining twelve thousand troops along the bank of the St. Lawrence. The French defensive line stretched east of the city for seven miles, between the St. Charles and Montmorency Rivers. Montcalm hoped that these forces would prevent the British from land-ing below the city. The French general understood that he did not have to defeat the British in battle in order to claim victo-ry. He only needed to hold the city until October, when the arrival of winter would force the British to leave the area. Montcalm believed that if he defended Quebec successfully, the British would have to negotiate a peace treaty with France.

Meanwhile, Wolfe struggled to prepare his men for the expedition. Many of his troops came down with measles dur-ing their voyage from England. The general thus ended up sail-ing for Louisbourg with only eighty-five hundred men, rather than twelve thousand. Nevertheless, Wolfe's expedition sailed up the St. Lawrence on June 5. In order to confuse the people on shore, the British ships flew French flags. The Canadians were delighted to see French ships entering the river. Several pilots rowed out to meet the ships and help them make their way through the tricky entrance to the river. As soon as the pi-lots came on board, however, the British revealed their true identity and forced the pilots to cooperate at gunpoint.

The British fleet arrived at Quebec on June 26. They set up a base camp on the Île d'Orléans, a large island in the middle of the St. Lawrence about four miles below the city. When Wolfe saw the strategic location of the city and the im-pressive French defenses for the first time, he worried that he was about to attack "the strongest country in the world." A short time after the British fleet arrived, the governor of New France, Pierre François de Rigaud, marquis de Vaudreuil (1698–1778; see box in chapter 5), ordered French troops to launch a sneak attack in hopes of chasing them away. Small groups of French soldiers towed boats full of explosives to-ward the anchored British ships in the middle of the night. Then they lit the boats on fire and rowed away quickly. But alert British sailors managed to row their own boats out and turn the burning boats around before they could damage the fleet. Montcalm reacted calmly when he heard about the mis-sion's failure. He had not supported the plan and had actual-ly expected it to fail.

On June 29, British soldiers climbed the cliffs at Point Levis, directly across the river from Quebec. They built fortifi-cations on top of the cliff and hauled up cannons. On July 9, Wolfe ordered an attack on the east side of the French line,

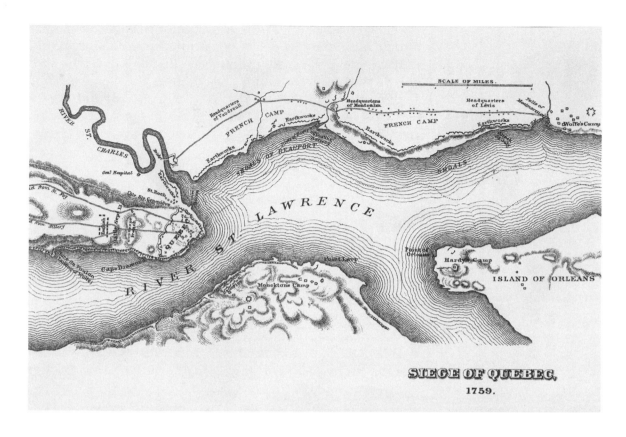

near the Montmorency River. British ships fired cannons to create a landing area for British troops, but the soldiers were turned back by heavy French gunfire. On July 12, the British forces began firing artillery shells from Point Levis into the city of Quebec. This bombing would continue off and on for the next two months. Some of the shells set fire to buildings and forced residents to leave their homes. On July 31, Wolfe ordered another attack on the French lines below the city. Once again, the French defenses turned back the attack, killing 210 British soldiers and wounding 200 more in the process.

A 1759 map of the siege of Quebec. *Reproduced by permission of the Corbis Corporation.*

Wolfe launches a desperate attack

Wolfe grew more and more frustrated at his inability to land troops on shore and set up a siege of Quebec. Like Montcalm, he understood that time was on the side of the French. At the first hint of winter, the British fleet would be forced to withdraw from the St. Lawrence, ending the expedition. Wolfe knew that his best hope of capturing Quebec would be to draw his enemy out of the city and into battle. He even sent British troops to conduct violent raids in the Canadian countryside, destroying fourteen hundred farms during the month of August. But Montcalm refused to allow Wolfe to provoke him into battle. "My antagonist [enemy] has wisely shut himself up in inaccessible entrenchments [defensive positions that are difficult to reach], so that I can't get at him without spilling a torrent of blood, and that perhaps to little purpose," Wolfe wrote in a letter to his mother. "The Marquis de Montcalm is at the head of a great number of bad soldiers, and I am at the head of a small number of good ones, that wish for nothing so much as to fight him—but the wary old fellow avoids an action doubtful of the behavior of his army."

Another factor in Wolfe's frustration was his declining health. He suffered from painful kidney stones, as well as a terrible fever and cough. As he grew weaker, Wolfe became convinced that he was going to die. He decided that he would rather die a glorious death on the field of battle than die slowly from disease. Desperate to earn a reputation as a brilliant general before he died, Wolfe began planning a final attack on the French lines. This time, the British troops would attempt to land west of Quebec at a spot called L'Anse au Foulon, which later became known as Wolfe's Cove. An overgrown footpath led from the cove to the top of the cliffs a short distance upriver from the city. This path could give the British access to the Plains of Abraham, broad fields that stretched behind Quebec and provided an ideal place to set up a siege.

Historians have long wondered how Wolfe decided where to launch his attack. One story says that Wolfe spotted the path leading up the cliffs while scanning the French defenses through a telescope. Some historians claim that Wolfe learned about the path from Captain Robert Stobo (1727–c. 1772; see box in chapter 4), a British soldier who had been held in Quebec as a prisoner of war for several years and had recently escaped. Other historians think that corrupt French officials told Wolfe about the path because Montcalm was about to expose their illegal activities.

Wolfe chose to launch the attack on the night of September 12. Part of the British fleet bombed the coast east of the city in order to confuse the French. Meanwhile, the remaining

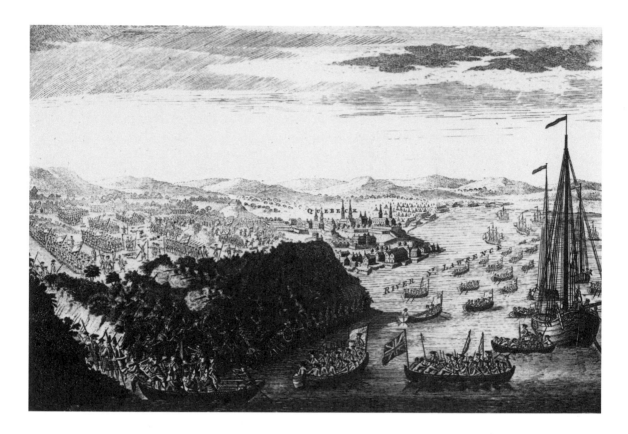

British ships slipped past Quebec and dropped off 5,000 troops in Wolfe's Cove. These troops scrambled up the path to the top of the 175-foot cliff and quickly overtook a small group of French guards. Then they moved onto the Plains of Abraham and arranged themselves in battle formation.

Montcalm was fooled at first by the British action east of Quebec. By the time he arrived in the city itself, Wolfe had already moved his troops onto the field of battle. The French general decided to engage the British forces in battle before they had a chance to dig trenches and set up a siege. But Montcalm had only forty-five hundred troops with him, and they had less training and discipline than the British forces. In fact, many of the British troops facing him on the Plains had taken part in the 1758 campaigns and were among the most experienced soldiers in North America at that time.

As Montcalm's army crossed the Plains to begin the battle, Wolfe's forces stood their ground and waited until the enemy came within firing range. Then the British opened fire

British forces exchange fire with Canadian militia in Quebec, while British and French armies meet on the Plains of Abraham.
Reproduced by permission of Getty Images.

British general James Wolfe lies dying in the arms of his compatriots following the siege of Quebec. *Reproduced by permission of Getty Images.*

and devastated the French troops. Montcalm and most of his officers were killed, and approximately fourteen hundred French soldiers were killed or wounded. The inexperienced French troops then turned around and fled back toward the walls of the city. The British troops started to chase after them, but then Canadian and Indian forces opened fire from hidden positions in the woods and cornfields along the edges of the battlefield. Wolfe was seriously wounded and died a short time later. His second-in-command, Brigadier General George Townshend (1715–1769), called off the pursuit and gathered the remaining British troops together. Townshend got the British organized just in time to face two thousand French reinforcements under the command of Bougainville. Shocked to see that Montcalm had been defeated, Bougainville briefly exchanged fire with the British troops and then withdrew his forces from the battlefield.

Once the French troops had retreated, the British forces began digging trenches and preparing for a siege. Inside the city walls, the French troops and Canadian residents lacked leadership and direction without Montcalm. They became discouraged and worried. Governor Vaudreuil soon left Quebec with most of the remaining French troops. On September 18, the few remaining Canadians surrendered Quebec to the British. Townshend gave the Canadians generous terms of surrender that allowed residents to remain in the city if they swore an oath of loyalty to Great Britain. Then the British Navy sailed down the St. Lawrence and out to sea, leaving seven thousand British troops under Brigadier General James Murray (1721–1794) to hold Quebec over the long winter. Although the French still held Montreal, the British capture of Quebec meant that the result of the war in North America was no longer in doubt.

Royal Navy wins the Battle of Quiberon Bay

As the French and British forces struggled for control of Canada, the war continued in Europe and elsewhere. The British failed to capture the Caribbean island of Martinique because too many British sailors fell victim to tropical diseases. But they did manage to capture another French possession in the West Indies—the island of Guadeloupe. Valuable shipments of sugar and molasses from Guadeloupe helped the British pay for some of the huge costs of the war. In Europe, meanwhile, Prince Ferdinand (1721–1792) of Brunswick continued to push back the French, but King Frederick (1712–1786) of Prussia continued to face threats from Austria and Russia.

Perhaps the most significant battle to take place in 1759 was the Battle of Quiberon Bay. France had been planning to launch a naval attack against the British coast. After all, most regular British Army units had been sent to North America, leaving only poorly trained militia to defend Great Britain. Before the attack could take place, however, the Royal Navy engaged the French fleet in battle at Quiberon Bay off the coast of France. Admiral Edward Hawke (1705–1781) chased the French into the bay during a November storm. He then ordered his ships to attack at will, rather than trying to remain in battle formation. They ended up destroying or capturing several French ships and taking the lives of twenty-five hundred French sailors. In contrast, the British lost only two ships and three hundred sailors.

This pivotal naval battle destroyed the only remaining French squadron in the Atlantic Ocean. It thus ended the threat of a French invasion of the British coast. In addition, the victory allowed the Royal Navy to control the Atlantic until the end of the war. From this time on, the British fleet destroyed shipments of goods to and from France and prevented the French from sending troops to Canada. The combination of all of these British successes led people in England to call 1759 "the year of miracles."

1760–62: The War Continues in Europe

8

By capturing Quebec, the capital city of New France, the British had reduced French territory in North America to Montreal and a few scattered forts in the Great Lakes region. As 1760 began, British leaders felt fairly confident that they would win the French and Indian War (1754–63; known in Europe as the Seven Years' War). British secretary of state **William Pitt** (1708–1788; see entry) gave his top North American general, **Jeffery Amherst** (1717–1797; see entry), a great deal of freedom to develop a plan to capture Montreal and seal the victory.

French surrender Montreal

Amherst came up with a three-part plan to complete the invasion of Canada. He decided to send three separate armies toward Montreal from different directions. Brigadier General James Murray (c. 1721–1794) would move west up the St. Lawrence River from Quebec with four thousand troops. Brigadier General William Haviland would work his way north across Lake Champlain with thirty-five hundred

Words to Know

Ohio Country: A vast wilderness that stretched from the Great Lakes in the north to the Ohio River in the south, and from the Allegheny Mountains in the east to the Mississippi River in the west; the French and British fought for control of this region, which lay between the French and British colonies in North America.

Siege: A military strategy that involves surrounding a target, cutting it off from outside help and supplies, and using artillery to break down its defenses.

men. Amherst himself would lead twelve thousand men—including one thousand Iroquois warriors—east across Lake Ontario. Amherst hoped that all of these armies would gather in the city at the same time, trapping the French troops and forcing them to surrender.

Before Amherst could put his plan into action, however, the French made one last desperate move. In the early spring of 1760, François-Gaston, chevalier de Levis (1720–1787)—who had taken charge of the French forces after the former commander, **Louis-Joseph, marquis de Montcalm-Gozon de Saint-Véran** (1712–1759; see entry), was killed—tried to recapture Quebec. Levis led more than seven thousand men, including some Canadian refugees who had left the city when the British took over. The French forces advanced on the city, where British troops under Murray had spent a long and difficult winter. About one thousand of Murray's seven thousand troops had died from cold, hunger, or disease, and two thousand more were too ill or weak to fight.

Levis decided to set up a siege of the city on the Plains of Abraham, where the British had claimed victory the previous fall. Just as Montcalm had done with his French forces, Murray brought his four thousand British troops outside of the city walls to meet the enemy on the field of battle. Since the walls were still weak from British shelling the previous year, Murray felt that he should attack the French before they had a chance to set up their siege. But Murray's strategy failed. The French caused many casualties (killed or wounded soldiers) among the British forces and chased them back into the city. Levis then set up his siege of Quebec and waited for supplies and reinforcements to arrive from France. But these supplies and forces never arrived, because the British Royal Navy had established firm control over shipping on the Atlantic. The ships that arrived at Quebec in mid-May were British warships, and Levis was forced to retreat to Montreal with his French troops.

By early September, the three British armies had arrived at Montreal according to Amherst's plan. Levis brought his troops inside the city and prepared to defend it. He tried to convince the Catholic Indians (Native Americans) of the area, who had long been allies of the French, to help him fight the British. But the Iroquois warriors on the British side held a conference with the local tribes and persuaded them to stay out of the battle. In fact, some of the Indians from around Montreal acted as guides to help the British ships negotiate the St. Lawrence River.

Unlike Quebec, which sat atop high cliffs and was surrounded by strong walls, Montreal had few natural defenses and weak fortifications. The city sat on an island in the middle of the St. Lawrence and was guarded by a small stone wall and a few cannons. In addition, the British control of Atlantic shipping had prevented supplies from reaching Montreal. The soldiers and residents faced severe shortages of goods that forced many of them to leave the city. Under these conditions, Pierre François de Rigaud, marquis de Vaudreuil (1698–1778; see box in chapter 5), the governor of

People to Know

Jeffery Amherst (1717–1797): British military leader who became commander-in-chief of British forces in North America in 1758 and led the siege of Louisbourg and capture of Montreal.

John Stuart, third earl of Bute (1713–1792): British political leader who forced William Pitt to resign; served as prime minister of Great Britain, 1761–63.

King George III (1738–1820): King of England, 1760–1820; after claiming the throne near the end of the French and Indian War, his policies created resistance in the American colonies that led to the American Revolution.

James Murray (c. 1721–1794): British general who served under James Wolfe during the Battle of Quebec and went on to serve as the first British governor of Canada, 1764–68.

William Pitt (1708–1788): British political leader who took control of the North American war effort in 1757; his policies gained the support of the American colonists.

New France, decided that Montreal could not be defended. He surrendered the city to Amherst on September 8, 1760. A week later, the final French fort in Detroit surrendered to **Robert Rogers** (1731–1795; see entry), leader of a group of American wilderness fighters called rangers. This event marked the end of the French and Indian War in North America, six years after it had begun. It also meant that the French colony of New France ceased to exist after 150 years.

Trader George Croghan Predicts Indian Wars

For many years before the French and Indian War, Indians had enjoyed fair trading arrangements with the French that helped both sides become more prosperous. Over time, the Indians came to depend on certain goods they acquired from the French. For example, many tribes used guns and ammunition—rather than bows and arrows—for hunting and for defending themselves against their enemies.

When British armies needed to gain the support of the Indians in their struggle with the French for control of North America, they continued many of the French trading practices. But after the war ended in North America, British General Jeffery Amherst placed restrictions on the trade between Indian nations and British settlers. Amherst prohibited the sale of alcohol to Indians and the giving of gifts to encourage

Indian cooperation, and he strictly limited the number of guns and amount of ammunition Indians could receive.

Amherst thought these policies would help make the frontier less dangerous for British settlers, but in fact they had the opposite effect. Many tribes fought against the new rules by conducting violent raids on British settlements.

George Croghan, an Irish immigrant who had settled in Pennsylvania, was one of the first British traders to do business in the Ohio Country. He opened a trading post on the site of present-day Cleveland in 1747, several years before the war began. Based on his long experience trading among the Indians of the Ohio Country, Croghan warned British leaders that Amherst's policies would create problems:

Conflicts with Indians continue on the frontier

News of the British victory in Canada was celebrated throughout the American colonies. Thousands of colonists began streaming across the Allegheny Mountains to settle the new lands to the west, confident that they no longer had to worry about attacks from the French or their Indian allies. In fact, large communities of settlers formed around many of the British forts and trading posts in the Ohio Country. General Amherst encouraged these settlers. After all, British leaders were recalling many of his regular soldiers to fight in the ongoing war in Europe. He hoped that settlers could help his remaining colonial troops secure the conquered territory.

Lieutenant Colonel George Croghan.
Reproduced by permission of Getty Images.

[The Indians] had great expectations of being very generally supplied by us, and from their poverty and mercenary disposition [tendency to fight] they can't bear such a disappointment. Undoubtedly the general has his own reason for not allowing any present or ammunition given them, and I wish [this policy] may have its desired effect. But I take this opportunity to acquaint you that I dread the event as I know the Indians can't long persevere [continue on their present course].... Their success at the beginning of this war on our frontiers is too recent in their memory for them to consider their present inability to make war with us. And if the Senecas, Delawares, and Shawnees should break with us, it will end in a general war with all western nations.

Source: Nash, Gary B. Red, White and Black: The Peoples of Early America. *Englewood Cliffs, NJ: Prentice-Hall, 1982.*

But the arrival of large numbers of British settlers angered the Ohio Indians. They felt that the settlers were crowding them off their land. In 1761, Amherst established a new set of policies designed to reduce the conflict between settlers and Indians and bring order to the frontier. He ended the practice of gift-giving, which had long been used by both British and French to gain the cooperation of Indians. He also placed restrictions on trade between settlers and Indians. For example, Amherst said that all trade had to take place at British forts rather than in Indian villages, which forced the Indians to travel long distances carrying heavy furs. He also prohibited British traders from selling alcohol to the Indians, and he limited the amount of gunpowder and ammunition the Indians could buy.

Amherst disliked the Indians and saw no further need for them after the British had achieved victory over France. He thought the new rules would make the Indians behave better and make the frontier less dangerous. But the Indians had come to depend on British goods for their survival. Some tribes had forgotten their old ways of hunting and needed guns and ammunition in order to feed their families. The Indians felt the trade restrictions left them defenseless against their enemies and made them more dependent on the British. Before long, a new wave of violence erupted as the Indians rebelled against Amherst's rules and struggled to maintain their rights and independence.

Some of the worst violence occurred during the Cherokee War of 1760–61. The Cherokees lived in the southeastern part of the American colonies and traded peacefully with the people of South Carolina for many years. In 1758, the Cherokee Nation even sent hundreds of warriors north to help British troops under Major General **John Forbes** (1710–1759; see entry) launch an attack on Fort Duquesne. But Forbes turned down their offer, to the warriors' surprise and anger. The Cherokees then headed home, only to be attacked on their way by colonial soldiers patrolling the frontier. Several warriors were killed in the ambush.

The Cherokee people felt they had a responsibility to take revenge for the death of their warriors. So Cherokee raiders attacked a frontier community and killed some white settlers. South Carolina Governor William Henry Lyttelton (c. 1720–1808) asked Cherokee leaders to meet at a fort to negotiate an end to the conflict. But then South Carolina troops took the Cherokee representatives prisoner, claiming they would release the negotiators only if the Cherokees who had murdered the white settlers came forward. The Cherokees responded by attacking the fort where hostages were held, killing the commanding officer. The remaining British troops at the fort then killed all of the hostages.

Outraged at the murder of their people, the Cherokees conducted a series of violent raids on white frontier settlements throughout 1760 and into 1761. They tried to convince other Indian nations to join them in an all-out war against the British, but no other tribes agreed. Amherst sent thirteen hundred troops under Colonel Archibald Montgomery to South Carolina. These forces destroyed several Cherokee villages, but were unable to follow the Indians when they retreated into the mountains. The Cherokees managed to capture Fort Loudoun on the South Carolina frontier and took the soldiers there captive. In the spring of 1761, the British sent an army of regulars under Lieutenant Colonel James Grant (1720–1806) to reclaim the fort and put down the rebellion. As the Cherokees ran low on ammunition, Grant's forces burned villages and killed many people. Cherokee and South Carolina leaders finally reached a peace agreement in the fall of 1761.

Seven Years' War finally ends in Europe

King George II. *Courtesy of the Library of Congress.*

Although the capture of Montreal had sealed the British victory over the French in North America, war continued to rage in Europe for two more years. During this time, the British government underwent an important change in leadership. King George II (1683–1760) died suddenly of a stroke in 1760, and twenty-three-year-old George III (1738–1820; see box in William Pitt entry) took over the throne. The young king relied heavily on the advice of his former tutor and closest friend, John Stuart, third earl of Bute (1713–1792). Bute did not like William Pitt and wanted him out of the government. But Pitt enjoyed great power and popularity because of his successful expansion of the British empire during the war. As the war dragged on, however, the military operations became so expensive that it pushed Great Britain close to financial collapse. Bute and the new king were eager to end the expensive war as quickly as possible. They worried that Pitt was willing to keep fighting indefinitely if he thought that Great Britain could claim more territory.

The difference in philosophy between Bute and Pitt became clear in 1761, when Spain agreed to form an alliance

John Stuart, third earl of Bute. *Reproduced by permission of Getty Images.*

with France. The agreement between the two powers said that if the war had not ended by the beginning of 1762, then Spain would join the fight against Great Britain. Bute viewed the Spanish-French alliance as a political scheme designed to push the British to negotiate peace with France. He was willing to talk about a settlement rather than face the possibility of expanding the war. Pitt, on the other hand, thought that the Spanish alliance meant that Spain definitely intended to enter the war. He favored declaring war against Spain immediately and launching attacks on vulnerable Spanish colonies around the world. When the king sided with Bute in this difference of opinion, Pitt resigned from the government in October 1761. But peace talks faltered, and Spain still joined the war on the side of France in 1762.

The British continued their military successes during this time by conquering French and Spanish colonies around the world. They captured French trading posts in India, seized French Senegal in West Africa, and took control of the French sugar-producing island of Martinique in the Caribbean. The British also launched successful attacks on Spanish possessions in Cuba and the Philippines.

At the same time, however, the war in Europe reached a stalemate. King Frederick II (1712–1786), leader of the British ally Prussia (a country that included modern-day Germany and parts of Poland and Russia), found his army surrounded and badly outnumbered by Russian and Austrian forces at the beginning of 1762. Then Tsarina Elizabeth (1709–1762), the Russian ruler who hated King Frederick, died and was succeeded by Tsar Peter III (1728–1762). Peter felt great loyalty towards Prussia and immediately made peace with King Frederick. With Russia's help, Prussia was able to defeat Austria by the end of the year. This remarkable turnaround enabled British leaders to withdraw support from their ally and use those resources in the fight against Spain.

Shortly after declaring war against Great Britain, Spain invaded its neighbor Portugal, which was a British ally. But the transfer of large numbers of British troops from Prussia and North America soon forced the Spanish to withdraw. The last major military operation of the Seven Years' War took place in September 1762, when British forces captured Newfoundland (located on the Atlantic coast of Canada) from France. The two sides resumed peace talks and settled on the terms of a treaty by the end of the year.

1763–65: The War Ends in Europe, but Conflicts Continue in North America

British and French leaders signed the Treaty of Paris in February 1763, officially ending the French and Indian War (1754–63; known in Europe as the Seven Years' War). The terms of the treaty reflected the powerful position that Great Britain had achieved over the course of the war. Great Britain gained control over all of the French territory in North America east of the Mississippi River, including eastern Canada and the Ohio Country. Great Britain also took possession of several other French colonies in India, Africa, and the West Indies. The British returned the sugar-producing Caribbean islands of Martinique and Guadeloupe to France, and in exchange they got back their military base on Minorca in the Mediterranean.

Spain, which had formed an alliance with France near the end of the war, turned over its territory in Florida to Great Britain. In exchange, the Spanish received the port city of New Orleans from France, and Great Britain returned the conquered Spanish territory of Cuba. Great Britain's ally, Prussia, made peace with Austria in 1763 by signing the Treaty of Hubertusburg. This treaty preserved the territory the two sides held at the end of the war, which was very similar to the territory they had held at the beginning of the war.

The Treaty of Paris was the most favorable treaty in European history. It gave Great Britain control over an empire that was larger than the one the Romans had controlled at the height of their power. Nevertheless, the terms of the treaty still came under criticism in London. Many people, including former secretary of state **William Pitt** (1708–1788; see entry), thought that Great Britain should be allowed to keep all the territory it had conquered during the war. They argued that Great Britain, as the victor, should dictate the terms of the treaty rather than negotiate with the French and Spanish. Public outcry over the treaty led to the resignation of John Stuart, third earl of Bute, who had forced Pitt out of office in 1761. The resignation of Bute, former tutor and closest friend of King George III (1738–1820; see box in William Pitt entry), created confusion in the British government, as various factions struggled for power over the next year.

Words to Know

Stamp Act: A law passed by British parliament in 1765 that placed a tax on all paper used for legal or business purposes in the American colonies; it met with violent opposition in the colonies and was later repealed.

Treaty of Paris: The 1763 agreement between Great Britain and France that ended the French and Indian War (known in Europe as the Seven Years' War); it gave Great Britain control over all the French territory in North America east of the Mississippi River, as well as several French colonies in India, Africa, and the West Indies.

Conflicts continue between Indians and British settlers

The fall of Canada had ended the fighting between French and British forces in North America in 1760. Yet conflict continued between the British settlers who moved into the newly conquered territory and the Indians (Native Americans) who had lived there for generations. When the French had controlled the territory before the war, the Indians had generally found them to be good neighbors. The French traded fairly with the Indians and did not try to settle on the land. In contrast, the British colonies sent thousands of settlers westward as soon as the war ended. These people often cut down trees, drove away game animals, and claimed the land

People to Know

Jeffery Amherst (1717–1797): British military leader who became commander-in-chief of British forces in North America in 1758 and led the siege of Louisbourg and capture of Montreal.

Patrick Henry (1736–1799): American political leader who first gained attention for his opposition to the Stamp Act as a member of the Virginia Assembly; later served in the Continental Congress and as governor of Virginia.

Pontiac (c. 1720–1769): Ottawa chief who united Great Lakes Indian tribes in opposition to British rule; led a large-scale Indian rebellion that resulted in the capture of several British forts before surrendering in 1765.

George Washington (1732–1799): American military and political leader who took part in the early battles of the French and Indian War and went on to lead the American Revolution and serve as the first president of the United States.

as their own. To make matters worse, British leaders placed restrictions on trade that prevented the Indians from getting ammunition and other goods they needed. These factors combined to make the Indians worry about their future under British rule.

The Indians did not think the outcome of the war should allow the British to claim their land. As **William Johnson** (1715–1774; see entry), the official representative of the British government among the Indians, explained: "The Six Nations, Western Indians, etc., having never been conquered, either by the English or French, nor subject to their Laws, consider themselves a free people." The Indians had not signed the Treaty of Paris and believed it should not apply to them.

This situation convinced an Ottawa war chief named **Pontiac** (c. 1720–1769; see entry) to take action against the British. Pontiac and the Ottawa people had already fought against the British during the war. They had helped defeat the army of General **Edward Braddock** (1695–1755; see entry) on the Monongahela River, and they had led raids of British settlements along the Pennsylvania frontier. Pontiac called a meeting of the Indian nations near Fort Detroit in April 1763. Representatives arrived from as far as a thousand miles away to discuss their concerns about the British.

At the meeting, Pontiac made a speech in which he criticized the Indians for becoming dependent on the British. He claimed that adopting the ways of the white man had caused them nothing but trouble. He called upon the Indians to quit trading with the British and go back to their traditional ways. He said he had a dream in which all the tribes overcame their differences and worked together. Pontiac concluded by challenging the other Indian nations to join him in launching an attack against the British invaders. "We must exterminate from our land this nation whose only object is our death. There is nothing to prevent us," he stated. "Why should we not attack them? What do we fear? The time has arrived.... Let us strike. Strike! There is no longer any time to lose."

Pontiac's Rebellion

Pontiac's plan involved attacking all the British forts located west of the Allegheny mountains at the same time. Most of these forts were small and isolated, and since the war had ended they were defended by very few soldiers. If his plan was successful, Pontiac thought the French might rejoin the fight. The Indians launched a series of attacks against British forts in mid-May. They succeeded in capturing many smaller forts in the Great Lakes region, including Fort Ouiatenon (near modern-day Lafayette, Indiana), Fort Sandusky (on the south shore of Lake Erie), Fort St. Joseph (near Lake Michigan), Fort Edward Augustus (site of modern-day Green Bay, Wisconsin), Fort Miami (site of modern-day Fort Wayne, Indiana), and Fort Michilmackinac (on the strait between Lakes Huron and Michigan).

Pontiac himself led one thousand warriors from various tribes in the attack on the largest target, Fort Detroit. Detroit was a compound that consisted of a strong fort, a trading post, and a hundred other buildings. The fort was defended by 125 British soldiers under Major Henry Gladwin (1729–1791), along with 40 British traders. First, Pontiac attempted a sneak attack. He asked Gladwin to allow his warriors inside the fort for a meeting, and the Indians secretly carried guns under their blankets. But Gladwin's Chippewa girlfriend revealed the plan to the British, and they had armed guards waiting when the Indians approached the fort. When his first plan failed, Pontiac surrounded the fort and set up a siege, hoping to starve the defenders out. British leaders tried to send troops and supplies to Detroit from Fort Niagara, but their boats were intercepted by the Indians. The Indians killed the British soldiers and sent their dead bodies floating past the fort as a warning to its defenders.

King Louis XV of France

King Louis XV (1710–1793) occupied the throne of France during the French and Indian War in North America. Born in 1710, he was only five years old when his predecessor, King Louis XIV (1638–1715), died. Louis XV was quickly coronated France's new king, but until he reached adulthood he was guided by Philippe II (1674–1723), the duke of Orleans, who served as regent (someone who governs when the rightful ruler is absent, disabled, or too young to rule). When Philippe died in 1723, André-Hercule de Fleury (1653–1743) emerged as Louis XV's main advisor. In 1725, the young king married a member of the Polish nobility, Marie Leszczynska (1703–1768).

During King Louis XV's reign (1715–74), France became embroiled in a number of wars, including conflicts in Poland and Austria. The most destructive war, however, was the French and Indian War (known in Europe as the Seven Years' War) with England. This clash first erupted in North America, where France and Great Britain became locked in a bitter battle for control of that continent and its rich natural resources. In the early years of this war, French forces gained the upper hand. But by the end of the 1750s, British armies were on the march against French territories all around the globe.

Alarmed at the prospect of losing the war in Europe, King Louis XV decided to keep most of his military resources in Europe rather than send them to protect the French settlements and outposts in North America. This decision ensured that the British and the American colonists would eventually be able to claim the continent for themselves. By 1760, most of the eastern half of North America was firmly in the hands of England.

In 1763, France ended the war by agreeing to the terms of the Treaty of Paris. This agreement established Britain as the world's leading power and reduced the

---

In late July, a heavy fog allowed another fleet of British boats, led by Captain James Dalyell (?–1763), to land safely with supplies and reinforcements. Shortly after his arrival, Dalyell decided to attack Pontiac's nearby camp. But a French trader slipped out of Detroit to warn Pontiac about the coming raid. The Indians ambushed Dalyell's forces while they were crossing a bridge over a creek, capturing one hundred British soldiers and killing or wounding sixty more. Dalyell was among those killed, and his mutilated body was left for the British to find.

King Louis XV of France. *Courtesy of the Library of Congress.*

influence of both Louis XV and France across Europe. France tried to recover, but its financial health had been ruined by the costly war and the king's own expensive tastes. The French people hoped that Louis XV would guide the country back to its former prosperity, but he failed to make meaningful reforms. For example, poor peasants continued to pay more in taxes than wealthy members of the nobility and clergy, and the government often interfered in the private lives of French citizens. The king who was once nicknamed "the well-beloved" had become a weak and ineffective ruler.

In 1774, Louis XV died of smallpox, and Louis XVI (1754–1792), his grandson, took the throne. But the financial and political mess left behind by Louis XV haunted the new monarch. In 1789, growing unhappiness with France's political, financial, and legal systems finally exploded in a popular revolt known as the French Revolution. This rebellion destroyed the French monarchy, replacing it with a succession of new governments that made many changes in the country's social, political, and economic fabric. Louis XVI, meanwhile, was imprisoned in the first months of the Revolution. He was finally executed on January 21, 1793.

As the siege of Detroit stretched into the summer, the Indians of the Ohio Country captured several more British forts. The Indians were unable to capture Fort Pitt, which was the strongest fort in the Ohio Country, but they surrounded the British stronghold and set up a siege. Without the forts to provide protection, British settlers along the frontier became vulnerable to Indian raids. Many settlers panicked and abandoned their homesteads for the safety of the cities.

As the extent of the Indian rebellion became clear, an angry General **Jeffery Amherst** (1717–1797; see entry) grew determined to solve the problem once and for all. Amherst gave his field commanders strong orders to attack the Indians and kill any they captured. He also suggested that they intentionally spread smallpox (an often deadly disease to which the Indians had no immunity) among the tribes as a way to reduce their numbers (see box in Jeffery Amherst entry). Amherst told his troops that the Indians should be treated "not as a generous enemy, but as the vilest [most horrible] race of beings that ever infested the earth, and whose riddance from it must be esteemed [considered] a meritorious [praiseworthy] act, for the good of mankind."

The first British forces to reach the Ohio Country were 460 troops under Colonel Henry Bouquet (1719–1765). They came under attack from the Indians near the Monongahela River, only a few miles from where General Braddock's army had been defeated by French and Indian forces eight years earlier. Bouquet learned from Braddock's mistakes, however. When Bouquet's forces had trouble fighting against Indians hiding in the woods, he ordered them to fake a retreat. The Indians emerged from the woods to chase the fleeing soldiers. Meanwhile, some of Bouquet's forces circled around to surround the enemy. The British claimed victory in the battle, although they lost fifty men and counted sixty more wounded. Still, Bouquet pushed forward and broke the Indians' siege of Fort Pitt on August 10.

Meanwhile, Pontiac's siege of Fort Detroit began falling apart in September. The Indians were running out of ammunition, and many warriors returned home in order to hunt for food to feed their families over the coming winter. Pontiac finally gave up the siege in October 1763. By that time, however, the Indian Wars had taken the lives of four hundred British soldiers and two thousand British settlers on the frontier. Upset over the continued unrest in the American colonies, British leaders recalled Amherst to London. They chose Major General Thomas Gage (1719–1787) to replace Amherst as commander of the remaining British forces in North America.

The following spring, Bouquet returned to the west with fifteen hundred troops and forced the Indians to return all of their white captives. In July 1764, William Johnson held a meeting with representatives of nineteen Indian nations at

Fort Niagara. Johnson agreed to remove all the restrictions that Amherst had placed upon trade, and in return the Indians agreed to make peace on the frontier.

British leaders try to control the colonies

Between the fall of Canada in 1761 and the Treaty of Paris in 1763, British leaders concentrated on the war in Europe and left the American colonies to deal with postwar issues on their own. Once the war ended in Europe, however, British leaders turned their attention to the colonies again. Throughout the war, British commanders Amherst, Braddock, and John Campbell, fourth earl of Loudoun (1705–1782), had complained about the Americans in the reports they sent back to London. The generals talked about the troubles they encountered in convincing the colonies to provide men, supplies, and money to support the war effort. They also discussed the poor training and discipline of the colonial troops. As a result, many British leaders developed a negative view of Americans. They assumed the colonies needed strong guidance and supervision from London in order to conduct their affairs. In addition, fighting the war in North America and around the world had cost Great Britain a huge amount of money. The British government struggled with heavy debts and a faltering economy as it tried to maintain control over all of its newly conquered territory. British leaders decided to address these problems by passing a number of new laws designed to establish firm authority over the colonies and collect taxes to help pay for the war.

But the British leaders did not have a full understanding of the situation in the colonies and how it had changed as a result of the war. They assumed the money they had granted to the colonial governments had paid for all of the colonies' wartime expenses. In reality, this money paid for less than half the cost of the war, and the colonial governments paid for the rest. As a result, many colonies were still struggling to pay heavy war debts of their own. American leaders felt they had already done their part to support the war effort. They viewed the British victory as the successful outcome of cooperation between equal partners. They did not understand why British leaders expected them to continue to

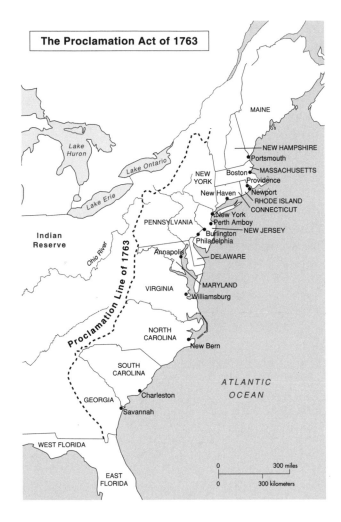

The Proclamation Act of 1763

A map of the eastern seaboard of North America following the Proclamation Act of 1763. The proclamation line shows that colonists were to stay east of the Appalachian Mountains, and the Indians to the west, thus avoiding Indian conflicts and continuing British control of the colonists. *The Gale Group.*

pay money and provide troops after the fighting had ended. In addition, the colonial governments had to deal with the rush of settlers westward into the Ohio Country and northward into Nova Scotia. The colonies argued amongst themselves about controlling the new territories and struggled to protect their expanding borders from Indian attacks.

The differences between British leaders' views and actual conditions in America led to disagreements when Great Britain tried to reestablish control over the colonies. The first step in this process took place when the British parliament passed the Proclamation Act of 1763. This act officially established new colonies in Quebec and Florida and opened them up for settlement. But it also set aside most other former French lands between the Appalachian Mountains and the Mississippi River—including the Ohio Country—as Indian territory. Although Great Britain claimed ownership of this territory, it reserved the land for the present use of the Indians and for the future use of the king of England. The act prohibited the American colonies from expanding westward. The idea behind the act was to prevent further conflict between British settlers and Indians by keeping settlers away from the frontier. Many Americans resented the Proclamation Act, however, because they thought the point of the war against the French and Indians was to make this land safe for British settlers. They felt as if their reward had been taken away.

In early 1764, British leaders began passing a series of new taxes on the colonies. The money collected through these taxes was supposed to help pay Great Britain's war debts and support the British troops that remained in North America. The American Duties Act, more commonly known as the

Sugar Act, placed new taxes on many items that were commonly used in the colonies, including sugar. It also included several measures designed to make tax collection more efficient. The Currency Act, passed a short time later, took away the colonial governments' power to issue their own paper money and use it to pay their debts. The idea behind this measure was to make sure that powerful London merchants received full payment for goods they shipped to America. But in reality, the Currency Act only made it more difficult for the colonies to do business amongst themselves.

Many Americans took exception to these actions of the British government. They felt no need for British troops to remain in North America, and did not want to pay taxes to support them. Most of all, the colonists objected to losing their rights and freedom in the face of tighter restrictions and control. Some people argued that British leaders could not impose taxes on the colonies without allowing American representatives to become members of parliament.

At first, opposition to the new policies was disorganized. Each of the colonies faced a different situation, so they tended to have different reactions to the new laws. In addition, the colonies still needed British help to deal with the ongoing Indian wars, so they were not willing to pick a fight with the mother country.

Riots break out in opposition to the Stamp Act

In 1765, however, the British government passed the Stamp Act, which placed a new tax on paper used in the colonies. Under this law, any paper that was used for business or legal purposes—including printed money, court documents, papers accompanying shipments of goods, and newspapers—had to have a small stamp printed on it. This stamp proved that the tax had been paid on the paper. Anyone who used paper without a stamp on it could be charged with a crime.

British leaders viewed the Stamp Act as a minor reform that would allow them to get a little more financial help from the colonies. In order to minimize opposition to the law, they gave the job of administering the stamps to promi-

Virginia assemblyman Patrick Henry, who led the protests against the Stamp Act. *Courtesy of the National Portrait Gallery, Smithsonian Institution.*

nent Americans. But as it turned out, this legislation created anger and resentment throughout the colonies.

Colonial governments began discussing the Stamp Act in May 1765. The government of Massachusetts was the first to express concern about the new law. Massachusetts leaders agreed to sponsor a meeting of representatives of all the colonies in New York in October to discuss it. But it was in Virginia that debate over the Stamp Act became most heated. Patrick Henry (1736–1799), a twenty-nine-year-old lawyer and new member of the Virginia Assembly, waited until most conservative members of the assembly had left and then gave a fiery speech against the new law. He sponsored a series of resolutions stating that only the colonial government had the right to place taxes on its residents. Henry argued that the British government had no right to tax the colonists without their consent. He also noted that the colonists could not give consent without having representatives in parliament.

The resolutions passed the Virginia Assembly on May 30, and Henry and his supporters left Williamsburg. The following day, conservative members of the assembly returned and attempted to repeal (officially revoke or take back) all of Henry's resolutions. But they were successful in repealing only the fifth resolution, which specifically addressed the belief that only the colonial government should have the power to tax its citizens. This resolution was considered particularly shocking because directly questioning the authority of the king in this way was practically unheard of at that time. Virginia's more conservative leaders worried that Henry's words might be considered treason (the crime of betraying one's country).

But Henry's ideas did not die, because his groundbreaking resolutions were soon published in newspapers throughout the colonies. In fact, some papers added two ad-

ditional resolutions that contained even stronger language against the Stamp Act and the British government. As Americans read about the Virginia Assembly's tough stand, organized opposition to the law grew among ordinary citizens. In Boston, Massachusetts, angry mobs destroyed the home of the man who had been appointed to administer the stamps and forced him to resign from his position. Then they went to the homes of other public officials and threatened to de-

A British Parliament Member Stands Up for the Americans

As the British Parliament debated about the Stamp Act in February 1765, many members spoke about the American colonies and their duty toward the mother country. One member of parliament, Lieutenant Colonel Isaac Barre, had spent time in North America and served under General **James Wolfe** (1727–1759; see entry) during the Battle of Quebec. Over time, Barre became fed up with what he felt were unfair statements about Americans made by his fellow members.

Barre then delivered a fiery speech in which he defended the colonists' loyalty to the king of England, but warned that the Americans valued their liberty too much to tolerate the Stamp Act. Barre's description of the Americans as noble, tough, independent-minded people made him a hero in the colonies. In fact, many groups that formed to oppose the Stamp Act borrowed the phrase "Sons of Liberty" from his speech. An excerpt from Barre's famous speech before parliament follows:

Your oppressions [abuses of power] planted them in America. They fled from your tyranny [severe authority] to a then uncultivated and unhospitable country.... And yet, actuated [moved] by principles of true English liberty, they met all these hardships with pleasure, compared with what they suffered in their own country, from the hands of those who should have been their friends....

They grew by your neglect of them: as soon as you began to care about them, that care was exercised in sending persons to rule over them, ... to spy out their liberty, to misrepresent their actions and to prey upon them; men whose behaviour on many occasions has caused the blood of those Sons of Liberty to recoil [draw back] within them....

stroy their property if they did not refuse to comply with the Stamp Act.

The success of the Boston mobs encouraged similar actions in other colonies. Many people decided that violent opposition was the best way to prevent the law from taking effect. Opposition groups called themselves "Sons of Liberty," a phrase taken from a controversial speech in support of the Americans that had been delivered in the British parliament by one of its members, Lieutenant Isaac Barre (1726–1802; see box). As the colonial governments struggled to control the mobs and reestablish order, each one ended up passing resolutions against taxation without consent. When representatives of all the colonies came together in the fall, they signed a joint petition asking King George III to repeal the Stamp

British parliament member Isaac Barre, who speak in support of the Americans. *Reproduced by permission of Getty Images.*

They have nobly taken up arms in your defence, have exerted a valor [shown

strength or bravery] amidst their constant and laborious industry [in the middle of their hard work] for the defence of a country, whose frontier, while drenched in blood, its interior parts have yielded all its little savings to your emolument [benefit]. And believe me, remember I this day told you so, that same spirit of freedom which actuated [moved] that people at first, will accompany them still…. However superior to me in general knowledge and experience the reputable body of this House may be, yet I claim to know more of America than most of you, having seen and been conversant [talked to people] in that country. The people I believe are as truly loyal as any subjects the King has, but a people jealous of [careful about guarding] their liberties … will vindicate [defend] them, if ever they should be violated.

Source: From the diary of Nathaniel Ryder. Reprinted in Proceedings and Debates of the British Parliaments Respecting North America, 1754–1783. *Edited by R. C. Simmons and Peter D. G. Thomas. Millwood, NY: 1983.*

Act. Despite the controversy, most of these measures were polite in tone. The colonial assemblies wanted to pressure the British government to repeal the Stamp Act without provoking them to impose their authority by force.

When the first shipment of stamped paper arrived in New York in October, thousands of people turned out to meet the ship and tried to destroy the paper. But the British troops that were stationed in the city managed to take the paper to nearby Fort George for safekeeping. When angry mobs surrounded the fort, though, Gage ordered the troops to give up the stamps.

British leaders were shocked by the violent opposition to the Stamp Act. They debated about what action to take.

They worried that repealing the law would reduce their authority over the colonies. But using force to make the colonists obey the law would turn the Americans into enemies. (The British parliament ended up repealing the Stamp Act the following year, although at the same time they passed several resolutions that condemned the colonists' behavior and emphasized their authority over the colonies.)

As British leaders considered their options, some Americans marveled at how the colonies had overcome their differences and joined together to oppose the Stamp Act. John Adams (1735–1826)—a Harvard-educated lawyer who would eventually become the second president of the United States—wrote several editorials for newspapers (often under the name Humphry Ploughjogger) about the new kind of politics he saw emerging in the colonies. "This Year," Adams wrote, "brings Ruin or Salvation to the British Colonies. The Eyes of all America, are fixed on the B[ritish] Parliament. In short Britain and America are staring at each other. —And they will probably stare more and more for sometime."

The French and Indian War's impact on American and world history

Although the French and Indian War is not as well known as some other wars—such as the American Revolution (1775–83), the Civil War (1861–65), or World War II (1939–45)—it played a significant role in shaping American and world history. In fact, some historians argue that the United States may never have become an independent nation without the French and Indian War. If the British and American colonists had not taken control of eastern North America from the French in 1763, then the thirteen British colonies along the Atlantic Ocean might have been surrounded by a vast, French-speaking nation.

Instead, the French and Indian War gave Great Britain a huge empire that it would struggle to control. The conflict also left France in a weakened position, holding little territory around the world and suffering under a mountain of war debts. This situation created a strong desire for revenge among the French people. As a result, the French provided valuable support to the American colonies in their fight against Great Britain during the American Revolution. In 1789, France's severe debts from the war and widespread social unrest flared into the French Revolution. This conflict, which eventually spread throughout Europe, reduced the power of the king and created an elected government in France.

War changes the relationship between Great Britain and its colonies

The French and Indian War created fundamental changes in the relationship between Great Britain and its American colonies. Before the war, British leaders had adopted a "hands-off" policy toward the colonies. Since the booming trade with the colonies helped make the mother country wealthy and powerful, they were willing to allow the colonies to govern themselves. But British leaders grew concerned about what they viewed as the colonies' lack of cooperation during the war years. They resented it when the colonies resisted their demands to provide money, supplies, and troops to aid in the war effort. They were also angry that some American merchants had continued to trade with France illegally during the war. Although smuggling goods across the border to New France was profitable for the merchants, it helped support the French war effort and may have made the war last longer than it would have otherwise.

These wartime experiences convinced many members of the British parliament that they needed to place the American colonies under firmer control. This idea gained even more support after the war ended, when settlers rushed headlong into the new territories and met with violent resistance from the Indians. Finally, the war had cost Great Britain a great deal of money. Faced with large debts and a slow economy, British leaders decided to place taxes upon the colonists in order to collect money to help pay for the war.

But the war had also changed the way many Americans viewed their relationship with Great Britain. Thousands of American men had served under British military leaders and alongside British soldiers during the war. Many of these men developed a negative opinion of the British Army. They

watched arrogant British commanding officers make poor decisions that sent hundreds of men to their deaths. They also witnessed many examples of the brutal physical punishment that was routinely used to maintain discipline and order among the troops. Over time, Americans came to believe that the British Army was not the powerful, unbeatable force they had once thought.

At the same time, many American soldiers played an important role in the British victory. They gained confidence in their own skills and abilities and felt as if they were equal to the British soldiers. For example, they noticed that American forces had defeated the French at the Battle of Lake George and in other clashes, while British forces had suffered several terrible defeats in battle. Yet the Americans found that British leaders did not appreciate their contributions and thought of them as inferior to regular British Army soldiers.

George Washington, a key figure in the French and Indian War, a courageous leader in the American Revolution, and the first president of the United States of America. *Portrait by Gilbert Stuart. Photograph by Michael Keran. Reproduced by permission of AP/Wide World Photos.*

Colonists' wartime experiences provide the foundation for a new nation

When British leaders tried to place strict controls and new taxes on the colonies after the war ended, their policies created strong resistance among the Americans. The colonists' wartime experiences had given them less respect for British leaders and military power, as well as greater confidence in their own abilities. Since they no longer faced threats from the French and Indians, they had less need for British protection and felt greater freedom to express their opposition to government policies.

Finally, the French and Indian War had created a generation of American men that had shared a common experience. They started to develop an identity as Americans, rather than as residents of a specific American colony. Several of these men emerged as leaders during the war. For example, **George Washington** (1732–1799; see entry) served in several important campaigns and led the defense of the Virginia frontier. He gained valuable skills and experience and was recognized throughout the colonies as a brave and capable military commander. When the American colonies fought for their independence from Great Britain fifteen years later, Washington proved his courage and leadership once again in the American Revolution. And—in what is perhaps his most courageous contribution of all—he loyally served as the first president of the United States.

Biographies

Jeffery Amherst

Born January 29, 1717
Kent County, England

Died August 3, 1797
Kent County, England

British general who led the siege of Louisbourg and the capture of Montreal

Jeffery Amherst was one of Great Britain's military heroes during the French and Indian War (1754–63; known in Europe as the Seven Years' War). In 1758, the young officer received a surprise promotion and was sent to North America to command a major military expedition. Amherst led the successful British attack on the fortified French city of Louisbourg on Cape Breton Island in 1758, which resulted in another promotion—this time, to commander-in-chief of all British forces in North America. The following year, he captured two important French forts on Lake Champlain and cleared the way for British forces to attack Montreal. In 1760, French forces surrendered Montreal to Amherst to end the French and Indian War and give the British control over North America.

Moves up the ranks of the British Army

Jeffery Amherst was born on January 29, 1717, on his family's country estate at Sevenoaks in Kent County, England. (Some sources spell his first name "Jeffrey.") He was the second son born to Jeffery and Elizabeth (Kerril) Amherst. He

Jeffery Amherst. *Reproduced by permission of the Corbis Corporation.*

123

joined the British Army in 1731, at the age of fourteen, and first served as a page (a personal assistant or servant) for a family friend, Lionel Sackville, the duke of Dorset (1688–1765). Ten years later, Amherst was appointed aide-de-camp (a top military assistant) to General John Ligonier. Amherst fought in Europe during King George's War (known as the War of the Austrian Succession in Europe) from 1744 to 1748. When the French and Indian War began a few years later, he was initially posted in Germany, where he helped collect supplies for British troops led by William Augustus, the duke of Cumberland (1721–1765).

The French and Indian War began in 1754 in North America, where both Great Britain and France had established colonies (permanent settlements of citizens who maintain ties to the mother country). The British colonies, known as America, stretched along the Atlantic Ocean from present-day Maine to Georgia. The French colonies, known as New France, included eastern Canada, parts of the Great Lakes region, and the Mississippi River basin. Both the British and French hoped to expand their land holdings into the Ohio Country, a vast wilderness that lay between their colonies and offered access to valuable natural resources and important river travel routes. But the Ohio Country was controlled by the Iroquois Confederacy, a powerful alliance of six Indian (Native American) nations whose members had lived on the land for generations. As Iroquois influence started to decline in the mid-1700s, however, the British and French began fighting to claim the Ohio Country and take control of North America. Once Great Britain and France officially declared war in 1756, the conflict spread to Europe and around the world.

In the early years of the French and Indian War, the French formed alliances with many Indian nations. The French and their Indian allies worked together to hand the British and their American colonists a series of defeats. In 1757, however, **William Pitt** (1708–1788; see entry) became secretary of state in the British government and took charge of the British war effort. Pitt felt that the key to defeating France was to attack French colonies around the world. He decided to send thousands of British troops to North America to launch an invasion of Canada. Like other British leaders, Pitt was frustrated by the British Army's lack of success in

North America. He felt that part of the problem was a lack of strong leadership. When Pitt asked his top military leaders for the names of talented young officers to direct the war in North America, General Ligonier recommended Amherst.

In January 1758, Amherst was called back to England to meet with high-ranking government officials. A few days later, he received a surprise promotion and new orders. "Mr. Secretary Pitt presents his compliments to Major-General Amherst," the orders read, "and sends him here with His Majesty's commission to be Commander-in-chief at the siege of Louisbourg." Many people were surprised that Amherst was selected for such an important mission. After all, he was only forty-one years old and had never led an army before. But Pitt recognized that the young officer had many good qualities. For example, he was well organized, calm under pressure, and believed in caution and methodical planning.

Leads the siege of Louisbourg and the capture of Montreal

Amherst soon set sail from England and arrived in Nova Scotia, along the Atlantic coast of Canada, in late May. His ships then proceeded north to Cape Breton Island, carrying twelve thousand British Army troops. Their mission was to attack Louisbourg, a heavily fortified French city that guarded the entrance to the St. Lawrence River. If the British forces could capture Louisbourg, then they could move up the St. Lawrence to attack the important French cities of Quebec and Montreal. Amherst planned to lay siege to Louisbourg. A siege is a military strategy that involves surrounding a target, cutting it off from outside help and supplies, and using artillery to break down its defenses. The first British forces landed on June 8, and a month later they had surrounded the city and begun pounding it with artillery fire. The British finally broke through Louisbourg's defenses and forced the city to surrender on July 26.

Pitt and other British leaders were thrilled by Amherst's success at Louisbourg. By the end of 1758, they had promoted him to commander in chief of all the British armies in North America. In 1759, British leaders planned a three-

Amherst and the Smallpox Blankets

Although the French and British signed a treaty ending the French and Indian War in 1763, the American colonies continued to face violent Indian raids along their western frontiers. Some of the Indians were lashing out in anger against General Jeffery Amherst's new policies toward the tribes. Amherst decided to use regulations and punishment to control the behavior of the tribes. The general placed restrictions on trade between British settlers and Indians and prohibited the giving of gifts, which had long served as a means of securing Indian cooperation.

Many Indians resented the new rules and became determined to resist British control. An Ottawa chief named Pontiac led an Indian uprising that led to the capture of several British forts in 1763. The Indians surrounded several other forts, including Fort Detroit and Fort Pitt, and placed them under siege.

Amherst was outraged to hear about the rebellion and decided that the only way to maintain peace on the frontier was to get rid of the Indians. He knew the British forces that were defending Fort Pitt against the Indian siege had come down with smallpox, a highly contagious and sometimes deadly virus to which the Indians had no immunity. According to *NativeWeb.com,* Amherst sent a letter to one of his field commanders, Colonel Henry Bouquet (1719–1765), in which he suggested that the defenders of Fort Pitt send blankets infected with smallpox to the Indians: "Could it not be contrived [arranged] to send the Small Pox among those disaffected [rebellious] tribes of Indians? We must on this occasion use every stratagem

part attack that they hoped would lead to the fall of Canada. While two separate armies attacked Quebec and Fort Niagara, located between Lakes Ontario and Erie, Amherst would lead a third army in an attack on Fort Carillon (also known as Ticonderoga), at the south end of Lake Champlain. Amherst and his ten thousand troops reached the French fort in late July and began digging trenches for a siege. The badly outnumbered French abandoned and destroyed the fort a few days later. After capturing Fort Carillon, Amherst moved his forces northward to Fort St. Frédéric at Crown Point on Lake Champlain. By the time the British forces arrived, however, the French had abandoned and destroyed that fort as well. In the meantime, British forces also succeeded in capturing Fort Niagara and the city of Quebec.

[scheme or trick] in our power to reduce them." Although it is not known whether Bouquet followed through on Amherst's suggestion, a smallpox epidemic affected many Indian nations around this time.

Amherst expressed his desire to commit genocide (the deliberate destruction of an entire race or culture) against the Indians in several other letters. For example, as quoted from *NativeWeb.com,* in a letter written in 1763 to **William Johnson** (1715–1774; see entry), the British official in charge of Indian affairs, Amherst discussed "measures to be taken as would Bring about the Total Extirpation [complete destruction] of those Indian Nations." He apparently did not have the same strong feelings about his other enemy. His correspondence shows that he considered the French a worthy opponent and wanted to treat them humanely under the rules of war.

Amherst's suggestion of sending smallpox-infected blankets to the Indians is one of the earliest examples of biological or germ warfare (intentionally using an infectious disease as a weapon). Unfortunately, there is some concern that the smallpox virus could be used as a weapon again in the future. By the 1970s, the disease had been virtually wiped out around the world. As a result, the United States and many other countries stopped immunizing their citizens against smallpox. However, samples of the virus have been preserved for the purpose of scientific research, so there is a possibility that terrorists might someday get hold of these samples and use them to spread smallpox among large groups of people.

In 1760, Amherst came up with another three-part plan to complete the invasion of Canada. He decided to send three separate armies toward Montreal from different directions—west up the St. Lawrence River from Quebec, north across Lake Champlain, and east across Lake Ontario. Amherst hoped all of these armies would converge on the city at the same time, trapping the French troops and forcing them to surrender. He led his forces—which consisted of twelve thousand men, including one thousand Iroquois warriors—to Montreal from Lake Ontario. As planned, the three armies reached Montreal by early September, and the city surrendered on September 8. This event marked the end of the French and Indian War in North America, six years after it had begun.

Indian policies cause a rebellion

As soon as the fighting ended and the British took control of North America, settlers from the American colonies began streaming westward to claim land in the Ohio Country. These settlers soon came into conflict with the Indians who had lived there for many generations. In 1761, Amherst established a new set of policies designed to reduce the conflict between settlers and Indians and bring order to the frontier. He ended the practice of gift-giving, which had long been used by both British and French to gain the cooperation of Indians. He also placed restrictions on trade between settlers and Indians. For example, Amherst prohibited British traders from selling alcohol to the Indians, and he limited the amount of gunpowder and ammunition the Indians could buy.

Amherst disliked the Indians and saw no further need for them after the British had achieved victory over France. He thought the new rules would make the Indians behave better and make the frontier less dangerous. But the Indians had come to depend on British goods for their survival. Before long, a new wave of violence erupted as the Indians rebelled against Amherst's rules and struggled to maintain their rights and independence. The largest Indian rebellion took place in the summer of 1763, when an Ottawa chief named **Pontiac** (c. 1720–1769; see entry) arranged for a number of tribes to attack British forts throughout the Great Lakes. The Indians captured several forts and placed several others under siege, until they were finally forced to surrender in the fall. In the meantime, British leaders grew frustrated at Amherst's inability to control the newly conquered territory. They recalled him to London in late 1763.

Amherst held the title of governor of Virginia until 1768, when King George III (1738–1820; see box in William Pitt entry) decided that the governor should live in the colony and asked Amherst to return to North America. Amherst resigned from the position rather than move to Virginia. In 1770, he was named governor of Guernsey in England. In 1775, as the situation in the American colonies neared full-scale rebellion, the king asked Amherst to serve as commander-in-chief of British forces in North America. Once again, however, Amherst refused to return to America and instead became a military advisor to the British government. He received the title of baron in 1776. Two years later, when France entered the war on the side of the Americans, Amherst became commander-in-chief of British forces in Europe. He retired from the military in 1795, and the following year he received the honorary rank of field marshal, the highest honor in the British Army. Amherst died in 1797, at the age of eighty, on his estate in Kent County. The town of Amherst, Massachusetts, is named after him.

For More Information

Amherst, Jeffery John Archer, Earl Amherst. *Wandering Abroad: The Autobiography of Jeffery Amherst.* London: Secker & Warburg, 1976.

Dictionary of American Biography. Reproduced in *Biography Resource Center.* Detroit: Gale, 2002.

Encyclopedia of World Biography. 2d ed. Detroit: Gale, 1998.

"Jeffery Amherst and Smallpox Blankets." *NativeWeb: Resources for Indigenous Cultures Around the World.* http://www.nativeweb.org/pages/legal/amherst/lord_jeff.html (accessed January 27, 2003).

Long, John Cuthbert. *Lord Jeffery Amherst: A Soldier of the King.* New York: Macmillan, 1933.

Mayo, Lawrence Shaw. *Jeffery Amherst: A Biography.* New York: Longmans, Green and Co., 1916.

Nester, William R. *"Haughty Conquerors": Amherst and the Great Indian Uprising of 1763.* Westport, CT: Praeger, 2000.

Louis-Antoine de Bougainville

Born November 12, 1729
Paris, France

Died August 31, 1811
Paris, France

French military leader who served in Quebec and later sailed around the world

Louis-Antoine de Bougainville. *Reproduced by permission of The Granger Collection Ltd.*

Louis-Antoine de Bougainville was one of the most interesting characters to fight on the side of the French during the French and Indian War (1754–63; known in Europe as the Seven Years' War). A promising mathematician who published an award-winning academic paper, he chose to pursue a military career. He served as the top aide to Louis-Joseph, marquis de Montcalm-Gozon de Saint-Véran (1712–1759; see entry), the respected commander of French forces in North America. Bougainville took part in the important French victories at Fort Oswego and Fort William Henry, as well as in the French defense of Fort Carillon and Quebec. His lively journals of his wartime experiences provide one of the best sources of inside information about the French war effort. Once the war ended in a British victory, Bougainville sailed around the world in hopes of discovering new lands to help France regain its former empire.

Serves as assistant to Montcalm

Louis-Antoine de Bougainville was born on November 12, 1729, in Paris, France. He was the youngest of three children born to Pierre-Yves de Bougainville and Marie-Françoise d'Arboulin. One of the major influences on Bougainville's young life was his older brother, Jean-Pierre, who was a prominent scholar with many connections in Paris society. Bougainville attended the College des Quatres-Nations and the University of Paris, where he studied law. After graduation, his brother arranged for him to study under several famous mathematicians. It soon became clear that the younger Bougainville had a great mathematical mind. In 1753, he published an important paper on calculus (a field of advanced mathematics), called *Traité de calcul integral*. Three years later, he was elected to the British Royal Society in recognition of his work.

But Bougainville was not content to stay in Paris and write mathematical papers. His strong sense of duty and need for adventure had led him to join the French Army in 1750. In 1756, he received the rank of captain and was sent to North America to fight in the French and Indian War. This war began in 1754 in North America, where both Great Britain and France had established colonies (permanent settlements of citizens who maintain ties to the mother country). The British colonies, known as America, stretched along the Atlantic Ocean from present-day Maine to Georgia. The French colonies, known as New France, included eastern Canada, parts of the Great Lakes region, and the Mississippi River basin.

Both the British and the French hoped to expand their land holdings into the Ohio Country, a vast wilderness that lay between their colonies and offered access to valuable natural resources and important river travel routes. But the Ohio Country was controlled by the Iroquois Confederacy, a powerful alliance of six Indian (Native American) nations whose members had lived on the land for generations. As Iroquois influence started to decline in the mid-1700s, however, the British and French began fighting to claim the Ohio Country and take control of North America. Once Great Britain and France officially declared war in 1756, the conflict spread to Europe and around the world.

Bougainville served as aide-de-camp (a top military assistant) to Louis-Joseph, marquis de Montcalm-Gozon de Saint-Véran, who was the new commander-in-chief of all French forces in North America. The two men traveled across the Atlantic Ocean to Canada in the spring of 1756. Although their voyage was rough, it led Bougainville to develop a strong interest in ships and seamanship that he would pursue after the war.

Helps the French win several battles

Shortly after his arrival in North America, Bougainville participated in the French attack on Fort Oswego, located on the southern shore of Lake Ontario at the mouth of the Oswego River (near the site of modern-day Syracuse, New York). Montcalm and his three thousand-man army captured two hills that towered above the British fort and aimed their cannons down into it. When Fort Oswego surrendered a short time later, Bougainville served as the translator between Montcalm and the British leaders.

In 1757, Bougainville took part in the siege of Fort William Henry, a British stronghold located at the south end of Lake George in northern New York. This time, Montcalm led eight thousand troops, including two thousand Indian warriors. They crossed the lake in small boats, hauled their artillery on shore, and began bombarding the fort. The British forces surrendered Fort William Henry after it was battered for several days by enemy shells. Once again, Bougainville acted as a translator as the two sides negotiated honorable terms of surrender. But the Indians were left out of the settlement and refused to accept it. They wanted to collect trophies from the battle—such as captives, scalps, weapons, and supplies—as proof of their courage. Their demands were rejected, and what followed has been called "the massacre of Fort William Henry." The Indians attacked the British survivors, killing as many as 185 men and taking several hundred more as prisoners. Montcalm and Bougainville were horrified by the Indians' behavior. They ended up paying ransom to free some of the British prisoners, and were reluctant to use Indians in their future campaigns.

In 1758, Bougainville participated in the successful French defense of Fort Carillon (also known as Ticonderoga), located on Lake Champlain in northern New York. About four thousand French defenders held off fifteen thousand British troops under General James Abercromby (1706–1781).

The French anticipated the location of the British attack and built a huge wall of logs and an abatis (a defensive barrier made from felled trees with sharpened branches) to block their approach. Abercromby sent wave after wave of British soldiers toward the fort, where they either became tangled in the abatis or were shot by the French. By the time Abercromby finally ordered a retreat, two thousand of his men were dead or wounded. Bougainville received a gunshot wound to the head during the battle, but he recovered quickly.

Following the French victory at Fort Carillon, Montcalm sent Bougainville back to France. The general saw a number of problems in the French war effort and hoped that his aide could convince the French government to send more troops and supplies to Canada. But French leaders wanted to concentrate on fighting the war in Europe. In addition, the British had won several important naval battles and taken control of shipping on the Atlantic, which made it very difficult to send supplies from France to Canada. When Bougainville sailed back to North America in the spring of 1759, he arrived just ahead of the British fleet that was coming to attack Quebec, the capital of New France.

Quebec was a difficult target for the British to attack. It sat atop high cliffs overlooking the St. Lawrence River and was surrounded by a large stone wall. As Montcalm prepared to defend the city, he stretched his forces along the cliffs for several miles upstream and downstream of the city. The general put Bougainville in charge of troops that patrolled the shoreline watching for signs of a British attack. The British fleet arrived at Quebec in late June, carrying more than eight thousand troops under Major General **James Wolfe** (1727–1759; see entry). They set up a base camp on the Île d'Orléans, a large island in the middle of the St. Lawrence River, just a few miles from the city. Over the next two months, the British forces made several unsuccessful attempts to break through the French defensive line.

Finally, on the night of September 12, Wolfe's forces used an overgrown footpath to climb the cliffs just upstream from Quebec. The five thousand British soldiers then arranged themselves in battle formation on the Plains of Abraham outside the walls of the city. Before the British could set up a siege, Montcalm led forty-five hundred French troops to face them on the field of battle. The highly trained British soldiers held their ground and soon forced the French to retreat back to the city. Both Montcalm and Wolfe suffered fatal wounds in the fighting. Bougainville, who had been patrolling some distance from Quebec, arrived too late to change the outcome of the battle. Quebec surrendered to the British on September 18. In 1760, Bougainville helped negotiate the French surrender at Montreal, which marked the end of the French and Indian War in North America.

Sails around the world

Once the British took control of Canada, Bougainville returned to France. He fought in Europe until the Treaty of Paris ended the war there in 1763. Under the terms of the treaty, France gave up most of its colonies around the world. Bougainville became determined to discover new lands and claim new territory in the name of France in order to help his country regain its empire. In 1764, he founded a French colony in the Falkland Islands, a group of islands in the South Atlantic that later became part of Argentina. He was forced to give up the colony a year later, however, when the islands were claimed by France's ally, Spain.

In exchange for giving up the colony, King Louis XV of France (1710–1774) offered Bougainville the opportunity to explore the Pacific Ocean. Bougainville set sail in November 1766 aboard a mid-sized French warship called the *Boudeuse,* accompanied by a supply ship called the *Étoile.* He hoped to become the first Frenchman to sail around the world. He also wanted to discover new lands and gather scientific information.

Bougainville and his crew sailed south across the Atlantic Ocean to Brazil, then circled around the tip of South America and entered the Pacific Ocean in January 1768. They landed in Tahiti in April of that year, and Bougainville described the tropical islands in his journal as "paradise on earth." While there, he unexpectedly discovered that one member of his crew was a woman. This woman, who called herself Bare, had disguised herself as a man to obtain work in Paris and kept up the disguise in order to have an adventure. She ended up becoming the first woman to sail around the world.

Bougainville sailed west across the South Pacific in hopes of finding the "great southern continent" (present-day Australia, which had not yet been discovered by Europeans) that many geographers thought existed. He came to the Great Barrier Reef, about one hundred miles off the coast of Australia, and almost wrecked his boat. Since he could not find a way around the dangerous reef and could not see land from there, he turned around. Bougainville went through the Solomon Islands and named one after himself, then continued on to the Moluccas Islands (or Spice Islands) and collected specimens of clove and nutmeg plants.

Bougainville returned to France in March 1769. Although he had made few notable discoveries, he had succeeded in becoming the first Frenchman to sail around the world. In addition, a young astronomer on his crew, Pierre Antoine Veron, had used new instruments to chart the correct longitude of many small islands for the first time. Bougainville published a famous account of his voyage in 1771.

Fights with the French Navy

In 1780, Bougainville married Flore-Josephe Longchamp de Montendre, a Frenchwoman from a noble background who was twenty years his junior. They eventually had three sons: Hyacinthe, Armond, and Alphonse. In 1781, France threw its support behind the American colonists in their revolution against Great Britain. Bougainville, who had remained in the French Navy after completing his voyage around the world, sailed to North America to take part in the war. He played a major role in the Battle of Chesapeake Bay in September of that year, which gave valuable support to the American cause. At the end of the American Revolution, Bougainville retired from the French Navy to write scientific papers.

Bougainville's long list of accomplishments led to a number of honors in his later years. In 1804, he received the French government's highest award, the Grand Cordon of the Legion of Honor, along with the title of count. Bougainville was also elected to the Academy of Sciences and the Board of Longitude. Numerous islands, mountains, and bodies of water were named after him, as was a variety of rose and the flowering ornamental bougainvillea vine. Bougainville died in Paris on August 31, 1811.

For More Information

Bougainville, Louis-Antoine de. *A Voyage Round the World*. London, J. Nourse, 1772. Reprint, New York: Da Capo Press, 1967.

Encyclopedia of World Biography. Gale: Detroit, 1998.

Explorers and Discoverers of the World. Gale: Detroit, 1993.

Kimbrough, Mary. *Louis-Antoine de Bougainville, 1729–1811: A Study in French Naval History and Politics*. Lewiston, NY: Edwin Mellen Press, 1990.

O'Connor, J. J., and E. F. Robertson. "Louis-Antoine de Bougainville." *The MacTutor History of Mathematics Archive*. School of Mathematics and Statistics, University of St. Andrews, Scotland. http://www-groups.dcs.st-and.ac.uk/~history/Mathematicians/Bougainville.html (accessed January 27, 2003).

Ross, Michael. *Bougainville*. London: Gordon & Cremonesi, 1978.

Edward Braddock

Born 1695
Perthshire, Scotland

Died July 13, 1755
Ohio Country (Farmingham, Pennsylvania)

British commander who led the disastrous
1755 Fort Duquesne campaign

British general Edward Braddock played a key role in the early part of the French and Indian War (1754–63; known in Europe as the Seven Years' War). In 1755, he arrived in North America with the full intention of chasing the French and their Indian (Native American) allies out of the disputed Ohio Country, a vast wilderness in the middle of the continent. But his first major military campaign against the French ended in disaster for the overconfident Braddock. His army was decisively defeated by a much smaller force, and the general himself suffered a mortal bullet wound.

Born and raised in a military environment

Edward Braddock was born in 1695, in Perthshire, Scotland. His father, also named Edward Braddock, was a high-ranking officer in the British Army. Little is known of Braddock's early life, but he was raised in a household that placed a high value on military service. At age fifteen, he en-

Edward Braddock.
Reproduced by permission of Getty Images.

137

listed in the British army's Coldstream Guards regiment, which was commanded by his father.

In the first years of the eighteenth century, Braddock took part in several battles of the War of the Spanish Succession (1702–1713; known in North America as Queen Anne's War) between England and France. Braddock rose rapidly through the ranks on the strength of his bravery and hard work, and by 1736 had achieved the rank of captain. He continued his professional advancement through the 1740s, earning praise in a variety of assignments for the British Crown. Braddock was promoted to major-general in 1754, the same year that the French and Indian War erupted in North America.

Though waged on North American soil, the war was mainly a conflict between Great Britain and France. Both of these countries had established large colonies (permanent settlements of citizens who maintain ties to the mother country) throughout the eastern half of the continent. The British colonies, known as America, stretched along the Atlantic Ocean from present-day Maine to Georgia. The French colonies, known as New France, included eastern Canada, parts of the Great Lakes region, and the Mississippi River basin. Both the British and the French hoped to expand their land holdings into the Ohio Country, a vast wilderness that lay between their colonies. This region offered access to valuable natural resources and important river travel routes. But the Ohio Country was controlled by the Iroquois Confederacy, a powerful alliance of six Indian nations who had lived on the land for generations. When the influence of the Iroquois Confederacy began to decline in the mid-1700s, the British and French began fighting to claim the Ohio Country and take control of North America. Once Great Britain and France officially declared war in 1756, the conflict spread to Europe and around the world.

A proud and stubborn general

By 1754, British leaders had become alarmed at events in North America. French forces over in the "New World" had succeeded in establishing alliances with a number of Indian nations. In addition, they had won a series of small clashes with British and American troops. Determined to turn the tide, Great

Britain decided to make General Edward Braddock commander-in-chief over all British and American forces in North America.

Braddock seemed like an ideal choice for the job in many respects. A veteran with forty-five years of military experience, he had repeatedly displayed his bravery on the battlefield. In addition, he was regarded as a tough and proud disciplinarian with a strong sense of duty. Braddock set sail for North America in December 1754, with two fresh British regiments. He arrived in Virginia in February 1755 and quickly assumed command of all British and colonial troops.

Braddock was immensely confident that his years of military experience in Europe would enable him to make short work of the French and Indians. He gathered the colonial governors together to explain his military plans. He wanted to attack the French forces at several strategic spots. In addition, he personally planned to lead a major military offensive against Fort Duquesne, an important French outpost on the banks of the Ohio River (the city of Pittsburgh, Pennsylvania, now occupies the place where this fort once stood). Braddock assured the governors that, with donations of supplies and money, he could have his forces ready to go in no time.

To Braddock's surprise and anger, however, the colonies provided few supplies or funds for the military effort. As weeks passed, the general experienced great difficulty in acquiring the provisions and laborers that he needed. During this same time, he showed a scornful attitude toward the capabilities of America's colonial soldiers, despite their superior knowledge of the surrounding wilderness and their familiarity with the Indians that roamed the Ohio Country. One of the few Americans who met with Braddock's approval was **George Washington** (1732–1799; see entry). The young Virginian served as a military aide to Braddock, and the British general expressed a high opinion of his bravery and intelligence throughout their time together.

Carving a path to Fort Duquesne

On May 29, 1755, Braddock departed from Fort Cumberland, Virginia, with an army of more than two thousand men. The force included more than fourteen hundred British soldiers, also known as "redcoats" because of the color of the long jackets they wore, and five hundred American soldiers from various colonies. The expedition also included a large number of supply wagons and massive cannons that would be used to attack Fort Duquesne, as well as two hundred engineers, laborers, and scouts.

Braddock intended to take his army westward over the Appalachian Mountains to reach Fort Duquesne. The army followed a faint trail through the thick forests leading into the mountains, but ax-wielding workers had to widen it every step of the way to make room for the big wagons and cannons. Every day, the army hacked its way through the deep forest, pushing up and down mountainous terrain. This exhausting work was made worse by summer heat and clouds of biting insects. On some days, the army managed to move only three or four miles from sunrise to sundown. All of these conditions combined to sap the strength and spirit of Braddock's soldiers. In addition, the threat of attack by hostile Indians or French forces kept everyone on edge. At one point in the journey, Braddock was approached by Shingas, an Ohio Delaware war chief who wanted to establish an alliance with the British. But Braddock coldly spurned the offer, and Shingas and his warriors left in an angry mood.

As Braddock's army moved ever deeper into the Ohio Country without being attacked, the troops began to think that the size of their force had scared away their enemies. Rumors that the French had abandoned Fort Duquesne swept through the camp. Braddock, though, ignored these rumors. In fact, he divided his army into two divisions. Eager to reach Fort Duquesne, he left the slow-moving cannons with the smaller of these divisions, and took the larger division—containing about twelve hundred British and colonial troops—forward. His plan was to use this larger force to surround the French fort, then attack once the cannons arrived.

On July 9, 1755, Braddock and his twelve hundred advance troops crossed the Monongahela River, just eight miles from Fort Duquesne. The general and his soldiers marched across the river as if they were on parade. The army band played marching songs, British flags fluttered in the breeze, sunlight glittered off gleaming gun barrels and bayonets, and the red coats of the British soldiers shone in the sun. Years later, George Washington said that the scene was the most thrilling sight of his life.

A few miles away, meanwhile, French forces were preparing a desperate defense against the large enemy force that they knew was approaching. The French officer in charge of Fort Duquesne, Claude-Pierre Pecaudy, seigneur de Contrecoeur (1706–1775), knew that the fort would fall if Braddock was able to use his heavy cannons. He knew he had to defeat Braddock before he reached the fort. With this in mind, French captain Daniel Lienard de Beaujeu (1711–1755) volunteered to lead an ambush. He planted about nine hundred French, Canadian, and Indian fighters on both sides of a deep ravine through which the British forces would have to pass.

Ambushed by the enemy

The first of the British to enter the area was an advance force of three hundred troops under the command of Lieutenant Colonel Thomas Gage (1719–1787). As Gage's men entered the ravine, Beaujeu sprung the trap. The Indian, French, and Canadian fighters under his command aimed a deadly barrage of gunfire from behind trees and rocks that covered the hillsides. Gage's troops tried to return fire, but they could not even see the enemy forces. As the Indian and French forces continued their relentless assault, Gage's forces retreated in confusion. They quickly ran into Braddock and the rest of the advancing British force. Riding back and forth on his horse, Braddock tried to restore order to his confused and panicked troops, even as musket fire continued to roar from the shadowy forest. Washington and others repeatedly urged Braddock to allow his men to leave the open road and take cover behind trees. But Braddock angrily insisted that his troops stay in formation in the middle of the road. His war experience had always involved armies that fought in neat formation, and he refused to believe that this European style of fighting could not prevail against wilderness battle tactics.

As the battle wore on, the Indians, Canadians, and French continued to fire away at the redcoats and Americans from their hiding places in the forest. The British and colonial soldiers tried to fight back, but most of the time they could only fire blindly into the woods. When American

Indians attack Edward Braddock and his troops as they prepare to march on Fort Duquesne on July 9, 1755. *Reproduced by permission of Getty Images.*

troops ignored Braddock's orders and tried to take cover behind trees, they were accidentally shot by their British allies.

Finally, after three hours of heavy fighting, the British and American soldiers fled in disarray. Braddock's military force, which he had believed was unbeatable, had been ripped apart. Musket balls had killed or wounded sixty-three of Braddock's eighty-nine officers. In addition, more than half of his army had been killed or wounded in the attack, while the French and Indian forces had suffered only minor losses. Braddock himself had four horses shot out from under him, and he received a serious bullet wound that passed through his right arm and into his lungs.

Braddock was carried from the battlefield to a safe area called Great Meadows (now the Fort Necessity National Battleground at Farmingham, Pennsylvania). Over the next few days, Braddock was in great physical and emotional pain. His wound made it very painful for him to breathe. In addition, he knew that the stunning defeat had left his military reputation in tatters. He had acted with great personal bravery throughout the battle, but his stubborn refusal to change his tactics had cost many British and American soldiers their lives.

According to some reports, Braddock recognized his error. Some accounts even indicate that he expressed regret that he had not followed Washington's advice and changed his military tactics in the wilderness. "We shall better know how to deal with them another time," he told one of his aides. But Braddock never had an opportunity to repair his reputation. He died from his wounds on July 13, 1755.

Several major historical figures survived the clash on the Monongahela River, including Washington, who would go on to become the first president of the United States; Gage, who commanded British forces during the opening battles of the American Revolution (1775–83); Horatio Gates (1728–1806), one of America's greatest Revolutionary War heroes; and Daniel Boone (1734–1820), the famous wilderness pioneer. But the battle, which came to be known both as the "Battle of the Wilderness" and "Braddock's Defeat," shocked British and American political leaders and ordinary citizens alike. Americans began to wonder if the British knew what they were doing, and the leaders of Great Britain were forced to admit that the war in North America might be longer and costlier than they had first believed.

For More Information

Dictionary of American Biography. Reproduced in *Biography Resource Center.* Detroit: Gale, 2002.

Hamilton, Charles, ed. *Braddock's Defeat.* Norman: University of Oklahoma Press, 1959.

Kopperman, Paul E. *Braddock at the Monongahela.* Pittsburgh: University of Pittsburgh Press, 1977.

Marrin, Albert. *Struggle for a Continent: The French and Indian Wars, 1690–1760.* New York: Atheneum, 1987.

McCardell, Lee. *Ill-Starred General: Braddock of the Coldstream Guards.* Pittsburgh: University of Pittsburgh Press, 1958. Reprint, 1986.

Sargent, Winthrop. *The History of an Expedition against Fort Du Quesne, in 1755.* Philadelphia: Historical Society of Pennsylvania, 1855. Reprint, Lewisburg, PA: Wennawoods, 1997.

John Forbes

Born 1710
Fifeshire, Scotland

Died March 11, 1759
Philadelphia, Pennsylvania

British military leader who captured
Fort Duquesne

John Forbes. *Courtesy of the Library of Congress.*

John Forbes led the British capture of Fort Duquesne in 1758. This fort was located in the heart of the Ohio Country (on the site of present-day Pittsburgh, Pennsylvania) and was vital to British hopes of controlling that region. Despite his poor health, which required him to be carried in a hammock strung between two horses, Forbes accompanied his troops as they cut a one-hundred-mile road through the wilderness to reach the fort. The general died just a few months after successfully completing his mission.

Sent to North America

John Forbes was born in 1710, in Fifeshire, Scotland. Little information is available about his early years. It is known that he trained to be a physician before joining a unit of the British army called the Scots Greys in 1735. Forbes fought in Europe during King George's War (also known as the War of the Austrian Succession), and was promoted quickly through the ranks. He became a lieutenant colonel in 1745, and was placed in charge of his own regiment in 1750. In 1757, he was sent to North America to fight in the French and Indian War (1754–63; known in Europe as the Seven Years' War).

The French and Indian War began in 1754 in North America, where both Great Britain and France had established colonies (permanent settlements of citizens who maintain ties to the mother country). The British colonies, known as America, stretched along the Atlantic Ocean from present-day Maine to Georgia. The French colonies, known as New France, included eastern Canada, parts of the Great Lakes region, and the Mississippi River basin. Both the British and French hoped to expand their land holdings into the Ohio Country, a vast wilderness that lay between their colonies and offered access to valuable natural resources and important river travel routes. But the Ohio Country was controlled by the Iroquois Confederacy, a powerful alliance of six Indian (Native American) nations whose members had lived on the land for generations. As Iroquois influence started to decline in the mid-1700s, however, the British and French began fighting to claim the Ohio Country and take control of North America. Once Great Britain and France officially declared war in 1756, the conflict spread to Europe and around the world.

In the early years of the French and Indian War, the French formed alliances with many Indian nations. The French and their Indian allies worked together to hand the British and their American colonists a series of defeats. In 1757, however, **William Pitt** (1708–1788; see entry) became secretary of state in the British government and took charge of the British war effort. Pitt felt the key to defeating France was to attack French colonies around the world. He decided to send thousands of British troops to North America and launch an invasion of Canada. Like other British leaders, Pitt was frustrated by the British Army's lack of success in North America. He felt that part of the problem was a lack of strong leadership. Pitt handpicked several talented officers, including Forbes, to direct the British war effort in North America.

Advances toward Fort Duquesne

Forbes was promoted to the rank of brigadier general and given command of a major military operation against Fort Duquesne. This French fort was located at a strategic spot known as the Forks of the Ohio, where the Allegheny and

Monongahela Rivers joined to form the Ohio River. Both the British and the French considered the Forks so important that the first battles of the war had been fought there. In 1755, British Army forces under General **Edward Braddock** (1695–1755; see entry) had marched from Virginia to the Ohio Country in order to attack Fort Duquesne. But they ran into an ambush as they crossed the Monongahela River and were badly defeated by the French and their Indian allies.

Forbes launched his own expedition against Fort Duquesne in the spring of 1758. His army consisted of forty-eight hundred American colonists and fifteen hundred British Army soldiers. One of his field commanders was **George Washington** (1732–1799; see entry), who had first visited the Forks of the Ohio on a diplomatic mission in 1753, and had witnessed Braddock's defeat there in 1755. Rather than follow Braddock's route through Virginia, Forbes decided to carve a new road through the wilderness of western Pennsylvania. His forces made a slow, careful advance toward the fort. They cleared a path through woods and over mountains, and they built supply depots along the way to help them hold the fort once they had captured it. Forbes also spent a great deal of time and effort talking with the Indians of the Ohio Country and giving them gifts to gain their support. Unlike Braddock, he understood the importance of having Indian allies, and tried to lure them away from the French.

Forbes overcame many obstacles on the way to Fort Duquesne. For example, he had to convince settlers along the Pennsylvania frontier to provide supplies for his troops, and he had to settle frequent arguments between his British officers and his colonial troops. But the most difficult situation he had to face was his own poor health. Forbes suffered from a painful skin condition that made it difficult for him to move, and he also caught a serious intestinal illness called dysentery. By September, the only way for him to advance with his troops was by riding in a hammock strung between two horses. Although the general was in tremendous pain, he managed to keep his forces together and inspired them with his courage and wit.

Claims the Ohio Country for the British

Forbes's troops had their first encounter with the enemy on September 14. The general had sent out an advance party of eight hundred men under Major James Grant (1720–1806) to scout the strength of the French forces defending Fort Duquesne. As the British troops approached the fort, French soldiers and Indian warriors came pouring out of the woods and attacked them. Washington and his Virginia regiment fought bravely and allowed the remaining British troops to retreat. Still, three hundred men were killed, wounded, or captured in the battle. Then the Indians who had taken part in the attack collected their trophies (scalps, captives, weapons, and supplies that served as proof of their bravery in battle) and went home, leaving only three hundred French soldiers to defend Fort Duquesne.

Learning that the French were running low on supplies, Forbes decided to wait and prepare for another attack. He ordered a full-scale attack on Fort Duquesne in late November. As his men approached the fort, however, they heard a series of explosions. The French had realized they could not defend the fort against the British attack and decided to destroy it rather than allow it to fall into enemy hands. Forbes's men raised a British flag over the remains of the fort on November 25, five months after the expedition had begun.

The following spring, the British began building a huge new fort at the Forks of the Ohio, which would be called Fort Pitt and would eventually become Pittsburgh, Pennsylvania. The success of Forbes's mission cut the connection between the French colonies along the Mississippi River and those in Canada and claimed the Ohio Country for Great Britain. It also helped convince some of the Ohio Indians to make peace with the British.

Dies shortly after completing his mission

Forbes immediately sent a letter to Pitt informing him of the successful capture of Fort Duquesne (as noted in *Letters of General John Forbes Relating to the Expedition against Fort Duquesne in 1758)*: "I do myself the Honor of acquainting you that it has pleased God to crown His Majesty's Arms with Success over all His Enemies upon the Ohio, by my having obliged [forced] the Enemy to burn and abandon Fort Duquesne." The general was then carried back to Philadelphia, where he hoped to recover his health before returning to England. By the time he arrived six weeks later, he was very weak and noted that he looked "like an emaciated [terribly thin] old woman of eighty." Forbes never made it back to England. He died in Philadelphia on March 11, 1759, and was buried at Christ Church.

Before he died, Forbes ordered a medal created for the officers who had served under him. As one officer later described it, "The Medal has on one side the representation of a Road cut thro an immense Forrest, over Rocks, and mountains.... On the other side are represented the confluence [junction] of the Ohio and Monongahela rivers, a Fort in Flames in the forks of the Rivers at the approach of General Forbes carried in a Litter, followed by the army marching in Columns with Cannon." The road that Forbes cut through the Allegheny Mountains, which became known as Forbes Road, eventually became an important route for American settlers heading west.

For More Information

Dictionary of American Biography. Reproduced in *Biography Resource Center.* Detroit: Gale, 2002.

Encyclopedia of World Biography. Detroit: Gale, 1998.

James, Alfred Proctor, ed. *Writings of General John Forbes Relating to His Service in North America.* New York: Arno Press, 1938. Reprint, 1971.

Letters of General John Forbes Relating to the Expedition against Fort Duquesne in 1758. Pittsburgh: Allegheny County Committee, 1927.

William Johnson

Born 1715
Smithtown, County Meath, Ireland

Died July 11, 1774
Johnstown, New York

British official who served as commissioner of Indian affairs in the American colonies

William Johnson was an Irish immigrant who became a prosperous trader in colonial New York. Part of his success was due to the strong relationship he developed with the Iroquois Indians of that region. In 1755, British leaders named Johnson commissioner of Indian affairs and gave him sole responsibility for negotiating treaties with the Indians. Johnson kept the Iroquois loyal to the British throughout the French and Indian War. He also served as a general, leading British forces and their Indian allies to victory in the Battle of Lake George and the capture of Fort Niagara.

Develops strong relationship with the Iroquois

William Johnson was born in Smithtown, County Meath, Ireland, in 1715. In 1737, at the age of twenty-two, he immigrated to New York in hopes of making a prosperous life for himself. Johnson started out by managing fifteen thousand acres of land along the Mohawk River that belonged to his uncle, Commodore Peter Warren. He leased small parcels

William Johnson. *Reproduced by permission of the Corbis Corporation.*

of land to other immigrants and helped them to build homes and farms there. Johnson also worked as a trader of furs and supplies for the settlements along the Mohawk River. He soon earned enough money to buy his own land across the river from his uncle's property. His land holdings eventually reached five hundred thousand acres. Johnson built a house on his property in 1742, and seven years later he established Fort Johnson there.

At the time Johnson arrived in North America, northern New York was the home of the Mohawk Indians. The Mohawk were part of the Iroquois Confederacy, a powerful alliance of six Indian (Native American) nations (the Cayuga, Mohawk, Oneida, Onondaga, Seneca, and Tuscarora) from the Iroquois language family. Johnson learned the Mohawk language and customs, and traded honestly and fairly with the Mohawk people. Over time, he gained the respect and friendship of their leaders. The Mohawk eventually adopted him into their tribe and gave him an Indian name, Warraghiyagey, meaning "doer of great things" or "Chief Big Business."

When King George's War (known in Europe as the War of the Austrian Succession) began in 1744, Johnson used his influence with the Indians to prevent the Iroquois Confederacy from forming an alliance with the French. In 1746, British military leaders gave him the rank of colonel and asked him to raise and lead an army of Iroquois warriors. Two years later, he was given command of the colonial troops raised to defend New York's northern border against French forces in Canada. In 1750, Johnson was appointed to the Council of New York, an important political group that helped set policy for the colony.

Becomes commissioner of Indian affairs

By the early 1750s, the Iroquois Confederacy found itself in the middle of a dispute between the French and British colonies in North America. The British colonies, known as America, stretched along the Atlantic Ocean from present-day Maine to Georgia. The French colonies, known as New France, included eastern Canada, parts of the Great Lakes region, and the Mississippi River basin. Both the British and French hoped to expand their land holdings into the Ohio

Country, a vast wilderness that lay between their colonies and offered access to valuable natural resources and important river travel routes. Tribes of the Iroquois Confederacy had lived on this land for generations. As Iroquois influence in the region started to decline, however, the British and French began fighting to claim the Ohio Country and take control of North America. This conflict, which started in the colonies in 1754, became known as the French and Indian War (1754–63). Once Great Britain and France officially declared war in 1756, the conflict spread to Europe (where it was called the Seven Years' War) and around the world.

British leaders wanted to keep the Iroquois Confederacy on their side during the war. In 1755, they appointed Johnson commissioner of Indian affairs for the northern colonies. Johnson thus became the official representative of King George II (1683–1760) of England among the Iroquois and their allies. He was the only person authorized to negotiate treaties with the Indians. As he performed his job, Johnson usually acted as a trusted advisor to Iroquois leaders. He kept them informed of British plans and tried to convince them to support the British war effort. He also tried to prevent the colonists from cheating the Indians in trade or tricking them into giving up their land. His efforts helped keep the Iroquois loyal to Great Britain throughout the war.

Wins Battle of Lake George and captures Fort Niagara

Johnson also played an active role in the war as a military leader. In September 1755, for example, he led thirty-five hundred colonial troops and Indian warriors on a mission to attack Fort St. Frédéric, a French stronghold on Lake Champlain in northern New York. In preparation for the attack, Johnson transported his men and supplies to Lake George, where he set up camp. Before Johnson could move against Fort St. Frédéric, however, he came under attack from French and Indian forces under Baron Ludwig August (also known as Jean-Armand) Dieskau (1701–1767). In what became known as the Battle of Lake George, Johnson's forces turned back the French attack and even managed to capture Dieskau. Even though he had never threatened Fort St.

Frédéric, Johnson was hailed as a hero afterward. After all, it was the first important British victory of the war, and it also stopped the French from advancing into New York. Johnson received a monetary reward and the title of baron from King George II in recognition of his efforts.

Once the British turned the tide of the war in their favor with a series of important victories in 1758, Johnson found it easier to convince the Indians to join the fight. In 1759, he gathered one thousand Indian warriors to take part in the British attack on Fort Niagara. They joined British forces under General John Prideaux (1718–1759) and reached the French fort in early July. The British forces then set up a siege of the fort, surrounding it and pounding it with artillery fire in order to weaken its defenses. Prideaux was killed in the early days of the siege, forcing Johnson to take command of the British troops.

A short time later, Johnson's Indian scouts informed him that French forces were approaching. The British forces built a log wall and an abatis (a defensive barrier consisting of felled trees with sharpened branches) to block the road to the fort. The enemy arrived on July 23 with a force of six hundred French soldiers and one thousand Indian allies. Before the battle began, the Indians on both sides held a conference and decided not to take part. The remaining force of six hundred French soldiers charged the British position in an attempt to break through to the fort. More than half of these men were killed or captured, and the others were forced to retreat. Fort Niagara surrendered to Johnson two days later. The capture of Fort Niagara cut off important supply routes between the French colonies in Canada and those along the Mississippi River, thus giving the British control over the Ohio Country and much of the former French territory to the west.

Deals with postwar Indian conflicts

Following the capture of Fort Niagara, Johnson resigned from the military to concentrate on his duties as commissioner of Indian affairs. Once the war ended in a British victory in 1763, settlers began streaming into the new territory that Great Britain had claimed from France. These settlers soon came into conflict with the Indians who had lived on this land for many generations. In 1763, several Indian nations staged a rebellion in which they took over a number of British forts in the Ohio Country and on the Great Lakes. The following year, Johnson held a conference at Fort Niagara and helped negotiate a peaceful settlement of the dispute.

In 1768, Johnson persuaded the Iroquois to sign the Treaty of Fort Stanwix. Under the terms of this treaty, the Iroquois agreed to give up their claims to sections of land in New York, Pennsylvania, and Virginia. In exchange, the colonies agreed to establish a permanent boundary for Indian territory—land that would be off-limits to settlers. After negotiating the Treaty of Fort Stanwix, Johnson concentrated on his own business interests. He founded the settlement of Johnstown, New York, which he turned into a community with its own school, doctor, blacksmith, and farm manager.

Johnson's health began failing during the 1770s, and he spent much of his time at home. But Indian friends and colonial leaders continued to approach him to act as a mediator in disputes over land. Johnson held his last council fire (a meeting of Indians to discuss important issues) outside his home in July 1774. He gave a speech to the gathered Indians on July 11, then went inside and died soon thereafter. His house, Johnson Hall, survived the American Revolution and still stands today. It was acquired as a historic landmark by the state of New York in 1906 and has been fully restored.

During his lifetime, Johnson was a member of the Society for the Promotion of Arts in America. He also helped found King's College, which later became Columbia University. Johnson was married three times. He married his former housekeeper, Catherine Weisberg (some sources say Weissenberg), when he was in his early twenties. They had three children together before she died. Johnson then married Caroline Peters, who was the niece of a friend, Mohawk chief Hendrick (c. 1680–1755). They also had three children together before she died. Johnson's third wife was Molly Brant, a young woman of Indian ancestry with whom he had eight children.

For More Information

Drew, Paul Redmond. "Sir William Johnson—Indian Superintendent." *Archiving Early America.* http://earlyamerica.com/review/fall96/johnson.html (accessed January 28, 2003).

Encyclopedia of World Biography. Detroit: Gale, 1998.

Flexner, James Thomas. *Lord of the Mohawks: A Biography of Sir William Johnson.* Boston: Little, Brown, 1979.

Flexner, James Thomas. *Mohawk Baronet: Sir William Johnson of New York.* New York: Harper, 1959. Reprint, Syracuse, NY: Syracuse University Press, 1989.

Hamilton, Milton W. *Sir William Johnson, Colonial American, 1715–1763.* Port Washington, NY: Kennikat Preess, 1976.

Igneri, David S. *Sir William Johnson: The Man and His Influence.* New York: Rivercross, 1994.

Moss, Robert. *The Firekeeper: A Narrative of the Eastern Frontier.* New York: Forge, 1995.

Pound, Arthur, and Richard E. Day. *Johnson of the Mohawks: A Biography of Sir William Johnson.* New York: Macmillan, 1930. Reprint, Freeport, NY: Books for Libraries Press, 1971.

"Sir William Johnson." *Johnstown, New York.* http://www.johnstown.com/city/johnson.html (accessed January 28, 2003).

Louis-Joseph, Marquis de Montcalm-Gozon de Saint-Véran

Born February 29, 1712
Nîmes, France

Died September 14, 1759
Quebec, Canada

French general who led the defense of Quebec

Louis-Joseph, marquis de Montcalm-Gozon de Saint-Véran, served as commander-in-chief of French forces in North America from 1756 to 1759. A brilliant general who inspired respect and loyalty among his men, Montcalm defeated the British at Forts Oswego and William Henry in New York. He also led the successful defense of Fort Carillon, despite the fact that his French forces were badly outnumbered. But Montcalm is best known as the general who lost the Battle of Quebec in 1759. He led a valiant three-month defense of the city before his French forces were finally overcome by British troops under General **James Wolfe** (1727–1759; see entry). Both Montcalm and Wolfe were killed in the famous battle that sealed the British victory in the French and Indian War (1754–63; known in Europe as the Seven Years' War).

Shows bravery and earns promotions

Louis-Joseph Montcalm-Gozon de Saint-Véran was born on February 29, 1712, in Nîmes, France. He came from a military family that had fought and died for France for many

Louis-Joseph, marquis de Montcalm-Gozon de Saint-Véran.

generations. In fact, the family motto was "War is the grave of the Montcalms." Montcalm received a classical education before joining the French Army at the age of fifteen. He began his military career as a low-ranking officer in his father's unit, but was promoted to the rank of captain by the time he reached the age of seventeen. Montcalm married Louise Angelique Talon in 1736. In 1743, he was promoted to the rank of colonel and became a chevalier of the Order of St. Louis (the lowest level of French nobility).

Montcalm first distinguished himself as a military leader during the War of the Austrian Succession (1744–48; also known as King George's War). He fought bravely during the battle at Piacenza in northern Italy in 1746, was wounded five times, and then was taken prisoner by enemy forces. Upon his release the following year, he was promoted to the rank of brigadier general. Montcalm then rejoined the army in Italy and fought in several other battles before the war ended.

In 1756, Montcalm received the rank of major general and was selected to take command over all the French forces in Canada during the French and Indian War. This conflict began in 1754 in North America, where both Great Britain and France had established colonies (permanent settlements of citizens who maintain ties to the mother country). The British colonies, known as America, stretched along the Atlantic Ocean from present-day Maine to Georgia. The French colonies, known as New France, included eastern Canada, parts of the Great Lakes region, and the Mississippi River basin.

Both the British and the French hoped to expand their land holdings into the Ohio Country, a vast wilderness that lay between their colonies and offered access to valuable natural resources and important river travel routes. But the Ohio Country was controlled by the Iroquois Confederacy, a powerful alliance of six Indian (Native American) nations whose members had lived on the land for generations. As Iroquois influence started to decline in the mid-1700s, however, the British and French began fighting to claim the Ohio Country and take control of North America. Once Great Britain and France officially declared war in 1756, the conflict spread to Europe and around the world.

Hands the British several defeats

Montcalm arrived in New France in the spring of 1756. One of his main missions was to protect the water routes that linked Canada to French territory in the west. After drilling his troops daily for months, the general decided to launch an attack against Fort Oswego, a British stronghold located on the southern shore of Lake Ontario at the mouth of the Oswego River (near the site of modern-day Syracuse, New York). On August 10, 1756, Montcalm brought a 3,000-man army to attack the fort. His forces consisted of 1,300 highly trained French soldiers, 1,500 Canadian militia, and 250 Indians from six different nations. Montcalm and his army captured two hills that towered above the British fort and aimed their cannons down into it. One of the cannon-balls killed the British commanding officer, and the fort surrendered a short time later. Montcalm's forces destroyed the fort and took all of the boats, cannons, guns, and other supplies they could find.

Once the fort surrendered, Montcalm ordered that the surviving British soldiers be treated as prisoners of war and taken to Montreal. But his Indian allies had joined the fight in order to collect trophies—captives, scalps, weapons, and supplies—as proof of their courage. They became angry when they heard about Montcalm's plan for the British prisoners. The Indians ended up killing between thirty and one hundred British soldiers and taking many more captive. Montcalm was outraged by the Indians' behavior. In fact, he secretly paid ransom to reclaim some of the prisoners.

In 1757, Montcalm launched an attack on Fort William Henry, a British stronghold located at the south end of Lake George in northern New York. This time, Montcalm led 8,000 troops, including 2,000 Indian warriors. They crossed the lake in small boats, hauled their artillery on shore, and began bombarding the fort. After Fort William Henry had been battered by French artillery for several days, the British forces surrendered. Once again, Montcalm agreed to consider the British survivors as prisoners of war and transport them to Montreal. But the Indians were left out of the settlement and refused to accept it. What followed has been called "the massacre of Fort William Henry." The Indians attacked the British survivors, killing up to 185 men and taking several hundred more as prisoners. Horrified by what happened, Montcalm became reluctant to allow Indian allies to take part in his future campaigns.

In 1758, Montcalm led the successful French defense of Fort Carillon (also known as Ticonderoga), located on Lake Champlain in northern New York. About four thousand French defenders held off fifteen thousand British troops under General James Abercromby (1706–1781). Montcalm anticipated the location of the British attack and ordered his forces to build a huge wall of logs and an abatis (a defensive barrier made from felled trees with sharpened branches) to block their approach. Abercromby sent wave after wave of British soldiers toward the fort, where they either became tangled in the abatis or were shot by the French. By the time Abercromby finally ordered a retreat, two thousand of his men were dead or wounded. Montcalm was considered a hero for his unlikely victory.

Faces problems in the French war effort

Although Montcalm had managed to defeat the British in several important battles, by 1758, he was concerned about a number of problems with the French war effort in North America. For example, the French Canadian population was simply too small to provide enough food, supplies, and soldiers to defend Canada against the British. In fact, the British population in North America was ten times larger than the French population. Montcalm tried to convince the French government to send more troops and supplies to Canada. His pleas fell on deaf ears, as the French leaders chose to concentrate on fighting the war in Europe. In addition, the British had won several important naval battles and taken control of shipping on the Atlantic, which made it very difficult to send supplies from France to Canada.

Another problem involved Montcalm's relationship with the civilian (nonmilitary) governor of New France, Pierre François de Rigaud, marquis de Vaudreuil (1698–1778; see box in chapter 5). The two men did not like one another and disagreed over strategies for conducting the war, especially regarding the use of Indian allies. In addition, Montcalm was disgusted by the corruption he saw in the government of New France. He believed that Vaudreuil and his cabinet stole money and supplies from France that should have gone to the army.

In the early years of the war, Montcalm used his skill as a general to overcome these problems. His honesty, fairness, and bravery earned the respect and loyalty of his troops. At the same time, his careful planning and clever military strategies allowed him to win several important battles. But in 1758, the British government decided to concentrate its military strength in North America. The British sent thousands of troops and tons of supplies to its colonies and began planning a full-scale invasion of Canada. They won several important battles that year and pushed Montcalm's army back to the important Canadian cities of Montreal and Quebec.

The battle for Quebec

In 1759, the British decided to attack Quebec, the capital of New France. Quebec was a difficult target for the British to attack. It sat atop high cliffs overlooking the St. Lawrence River and was surrounded by a large stone wall. As Montcalm prepared to defend the city, he left two thousand soldiers within the walls of Quebec and arranged his remaining twelve thousand troops along the bank of the St. Lawrence. The French defensive line stretched along the cliffs east of the city for seven miles, between the St. Charles River and the Montmorency River.

Montcalm understood that he did not have to defeat the British in battle in order to claim victory. He only needed to hold Quebec until October, when the arrival of winter would force the British to leave the area before the St. Lawrence River froze. Montcalm believed that if he defended Quebec successfully, the British would have to negotiate a peace treaty with France.

The British fleet arrived at Quebec in late June carrying more than eight thousand troops under Major General

 Eighteenth-Century General Receives Twenty-First Century Funeral

Louis-Joseph, marquis de Montcalm's body remained buried at a convent in Quebec City for almost 250 years. In 2001, however, Canadian officials decided that the French general should be buried among his troops. His casket, draped in a French flag, was taken through historic Old Quebec in a horse-drawn carriage. The funeral procession also included a military honor guard dressed in uniforms from the 1750s and carrying flags from each of the units in Montcalm's army. The ceremony was attended by many important Canadian citizens as well as some of Montcalm's descendants. The general's new grave can be found in a small cemetery in the Lower Town section of Quebec, next to the graves of some of the men he led into battle.

French general Louis-Joseph, marquis de Montcalm lies dying after he was shot in the battle for Quebec in 1759. *Reproduced by permission of Getty Images.*

James Wolfe. They set up a base camp on the Île d'Orleans, a large island in the middle of the St. Lawrence River, just a few miles from the city. Over the next two months, the British forces made several attempts to break through the French defensive line. But Montcalm's forces held off the attacks and refused to be drawn out of their strategic positions.

Finally, on the night of September 12, some of Wolfe's forces used an overgrown footpath to climb the cliffs just upstream from Quebec. The five thousand British soldiers then arranged themselves in battle formation on the Plains of Abraham, a broad field that stretched behind the city and provided an ideal spot to set up a siege (a military strategy that involves surrounding a target, cutting it off from outside help and supplies, and using artillery to break down its defenses).

On September 13, Montcalm decided to face the enemy on the field of battle rather than allow the British to set up a siege. Riding on horseback and waving his sword, he led forty-five hundred French troops onto the Plains of Abraham. But the highly trained British soldiers held their ground and soon forced the French to retreat back to the city. Both Montcalm and Wolfe received mortal wounds during the fighting.

Montcalm was shot in the leg and abdomen. He ordered two of his soldiers to hold him upright in the saddle as he rode off the battlefield so that the rest of his army would not know that his wounds were serious. When the general finally got inside the city walls, a doctor told him that he only had a few hours to live. "So much the better," Montcalm replied. "I shall not see the surrender of Quebec." Montcalm died early in the morning of September 14, 1759. He was buried in the courtyard of a convent, in a hole that had been created by a British artillery shell, but was reburied years later (see box).

Quebec surrendered to the British on September 18. The British victory reduced French territory in North America to Montreal and a few forts along the Great Lakes. Both sides knew that the British were very close to victory, particularly since the French had lost their great general. Montreal surrendered to British forces in 1760 to end the French and Indian War and give the British control over all French territory in North America.

For More Information

Casgrain, H. R. *Wolfe and Montcalm*. Toronto: University of Toronto Press, 1964.

Chartrand, René. *Ticonderoga 1758: Montcalm's Victory Against Odds*. Oxford, England: Osprey Publishing, 2000.

Deziel, Shanda. "Montcalm Joins His Soldiers at Last." *Maclean's* (October 22, 2001): 24.

Encyclopedia of World Biography. Detroit: Gale, 1998.

Lewis, Meriwether L. *Montcalm: The Marvelous Marquis*. New York: Vantage Press, 1961.

Lloyd, Christopher. *The Capture of Quebec*. New York: Macmillan, 1959.

Parkman, Francis. *Montcalm and Wolfe*. Boston: Little, Brown and Company, 1884. Reprint, New York: Modern Library, 1999.

William Pitt

Born November 15, 1708
Westminster, England

Died May 11, 1778
London, England

British war minister during the
French and Indian War

William Pitt is known as one of the greatest wartime leaders in British history. He served as secretary of state in the British government during the French and Indian War (1754–63; known in Europe as the Seven Years' War). During this period, he directed British military operations and carried out political schemes with great effectiveness. Under his guidance, British and colonial troops added Canada and most other disputed areas of North America to the British Empire, and England established itself as the world's greatest power.

Privileged upbringing leads to a career in politics

William Pitt was born on November 15, 1708. His parents were Robert Pitt, a member of the British Parliament, and Lady Harriet Villiers, whose family was of English-Irish nobility. Young Pitt was raised in very comfortable surroundings and studied at England's finest schools. He attended school at Eton from 1719 to 1726, then moved on to Oxford and Utrecht in 1727. He suffered from a variety of illnesses as a

William Pitt.

youngster, so he rarely participated in the outdoor and sports activities that were popular with other boys his age. But he was an intelligent and curious youngster who filled his days with literature, art, and music.

In 1735, Pitt followed in the footsteps of his grandfather and father, taking a seat as a member of the Parliament, the supreme legislative body of the country. All across Great Britain, no laws or taxes could be approved without the formal agreement of the Parliament. In addition, only members of Parliament were eligible to serve as the prime minister or fill other posts in the cabinet. (The cabinet is a group of legislators who lead various government departments and serve as advisors to the prime minister.)

Pitt quickly established himself as one of the Parliament's most fearless and ambitious members. In 1736, he delivered a speech in which he strongly criticized the policies of King George II (1683–1760) and the government. The king was so angry about the remarks that he arranged for Pitt's dismissal from the "Blues," a ceremonial regiment of horsemen affiliated with the royal crown. But the move backfired. The British public sided with Pitt in the dispute, expressing admiration for his bold behavior.

From 1737 to 1745, Pitt served as assistant to Frederick Louis (1707–1751), the prince of Wales, King George II's son. During this period, he remained one of the most vocal critics of the ruling government. In May 1744, Pitt became seriously ill. He gradually recovered, but mysterious ailments and sicknesses dogged him for the rest of his life. In 1746, King George II permitted Pitt to return to the government, most notably as paymaster general of the military. In 1754, Pitt married Hester Grenville, with whom he eventually had three sons and two daughters.

Pitt guides Britain through the French and Indian War

Even as Pitt's political career flourished in the early 1750s, relations between Great Britain and France became dangerously tense. Since the late seventeenth century, these two European powers had repeatedly clashed for economic, military, and political supremacy around the world. In 1754, this struggle erupted once again in North America with the French and Indian War.

By the 1750s, both Great Britain and France had established large colonies (permanent settlements of citizens who maintain ties to the mother country) throughout the eastern half of North America. The British colonies, known as America, stretched along the Atlantic Ocean from present-day Maine to Georgia. The French colonies, known as New France, included eastern Canada, parts of the Great Lakes region, and the Mississippi River basin. Both the British and French hoped to expand their land holdings into the Ohio Country, a vast wilderness that lay between their colonies. This region offered access to valuable natural resources and important river travel routes. But the Ohio Country was controlled by the Iroquois Confederacy, a powerful alliance of six Indian (Native American) nations who had lived on the land for generations. When the influence of the Iroquois Confederacy began to decline in the mid-1700s, the British and French began fighting to claim the Ohio Country and take control of North America. This conflict—the French and Indian War—quickly widened into a global struggle.

When the French and Indian War began, Pitt repeatedly urged the government to attack France and its colonies all around the world. He called on the nation's leaders to increase the size of its army and navy, create a national militia, and send more troops to America. He also told his political allies that if he was running things, he could lead Britain to great glory. As noted in *Encyclopedia of World Biography,* he declared, "I know that I can save this country and that no one else can."

From 1754 through early 1757, British forces suffered a series of military defeats in North America and elsewhere. These losses triggered a political crisis in Great Britain. Finally, King George II called on Pitt to take leadership of the government, despite his personal dislike for the man. The king recognized that England needed to be led by a popular figure like Pitt if it hoped to win the war against France. Pitt gladly accepted the challenge, and in July 1757, he was formally appointed war minister of Great Britain. He shared political power with Thomas Pelham-Holles (1693–1768), the duke of Newcastle, but enjoyed authority over all of Britain's military forces.

When Pitt took over the war effort, England was struggling all across the world. The French and their Indian allies were scoring victory after victory in North America, and some British leaders feared that France was on the verge of seizing not only the fur trade and fisheries of that continent, but also the American colonies themselves. In addition, Great Britain had recently suffered military setbacks at the hands of the French in India, the Mediterranean, and Africa.

Reversing the momentum of the war

But Pitt quickly reversed the falling fortunes of the British Empire. He spoke with such great confidence and determination that he was able to renew Britain's commitment to the war. Indeed, his appeals to national pride inspired the English people. In addition, he proved to be an effective planner of military and naval strategy. He also used his authority to make sure the military received the best possible leadership. For example, he promoted and removed commanders based on their talent, skill, and bravery rather than their years of service in the military or family connections. Finally, he worked very hard to improve relations with the American colonists. During the first years of the French and Indian War, British generals and lawmakers had treated the Americans poorly. But Pitt behaved as if they were equals, and he listened to their wartime complaints and suggestions respectfully. As a result, support for the war increased dramatically throughout the colonies.

Under Pitt's leadership, England registered a series of major military victories around the world. In Europe, he sent huge sums of money to British allies so that they could expand their militaries. Before long, these armies were posting major victories over France and its allies. At the same time, Pitt sent large numbers of British troops to attack French outposts around the globe. In North America, for example, combined British and American forces swept through French territory in 1758 and 1759, capturing one fort after another.

In 1760, King George II died of a stroke and King George III (1738–1820; see box) took the throne. The new king's primary advisor was an old opponent of Pitt's named John Stuart, third earl of Bute (1713–1792). King George III distrusted Pitt and wanted him removed from office, but he knew that he could not immediately dismiss the popular Pitt. Indeed,

King George III—The "Mad King"

King George III was one of the most controversial monarchs in English history. Though considered an honest man of good intentions, there is no argument that he was a man of limited intellectual capacity. Historians generally agree that his minimal intelligence made him an ineffectual ruler and led to the controversy surrounding his tragic life.

In the first years of his rule, which lasted from 1760 to 1820, Great Britain seized control of much of North America in the French and Indian War. But he later lost the American colonies in the War for Independence, and he suffered from mental illness during many of his years on the throne.

Born in London on June 4, 1738, George III was the oldest son of Frederick Louis, the prince of Wales, and the grandson of King George II. He became king of England in 1760, after George II died of a stroke. In the first years of his reign, George III devoted much of his time and energy to restoring powers to the king that had been lost during his grandfather's reign. His main ally in this effort was John Stuart, the earl of Bute. In 1761, their opposition to an offensive against Spain led to the resignation of William Pitt, Britain's enormously popular war minister. In 1763, the Treaty of Paris, which ended the French and Indian War between Britain and France, established Great Britain as the world's leading economic, military, and political power.

In the 1760s, King George III appointed and dismissed a series of ministers to run the British government. He finally settled on Frederick North (1732–1792), the earl of Guilford, who served as prime minister from 1770 to 1782. But King George III and Lord North instituted policies that further increased tensions between Great Britain and its colonies in America. Relations eventually became so poor that the colonies launched a successful fight for independence and formed the

Pitt—known around the country as "the Great Commoner" because of his background in Parliament's House of Commons—had brought his countrymen a great deal of glory and honor. He had claimed most of North America for the British Empire, and French forces were in retreat all around the world.

In 1761, Great Britain and France initiated negotiations to end the war. Pitt, however, did not want to end the war. On the contrary, he wanted to expand the war by attacking Spain, which had allied itself with France. But when his advice was rejected, Pitt resigned from office in October 1761.

King George III. *Courtesy of the National Archives and Records Administration.*

United States of America. The loss of the colonies triggered a storm of political unrest that nearly forced the king to abdicate (step down from the throne).

In the meantime, the health and well-being of King George III became a major source of concern within the British Empire. In 1765, he had been confined to bed for three months by a mysterious illness that threatened to take his life. From that point forward, he suffered from periodic attacks of insomnia, hallucinations, excessive sensitivity to touch, and delirious behavior. Historians now believe that these symptoms came from a rare hereditary disease called porphyria.

The disease worsened in the late eighteenth century, and many British citizens, as well as King George III himself, became concerned that he might be going insane. During this period, his power and influence eroded significantly. In 1809, he became blind, and two years later his mental state became so unbalanced that he could no longer function as king. His son, who later became George IV (1762–1830), acted as regent (someone who rules during the disability or absence of a king or other ruler) until George III's death on January 29, 1820.

Two years later, France and England signed the Treaty of Paris, which ended the French and Indian War. Pitt bitterly criticized the treaty, but it firmly established Britain as the world's great economic, commercial, and colonial power.

Hampered by failing health

Pitt struggled with a range of health problems through the early 1760s. He spent most of this time at his country estate in Bath, England. Every once in a while, he would travel to London, where his public proclamations on government policies continued to attract attention. For example, he repeatedly expressed his opposition to imposing taxes on the American colonies since they were not represented in the British Parliament. He believed that this "taxation without representation" was illegal, according to British law. At the same time, however, he made it very clear that he considered the colonies a part of the British Empire.

In August 1766, the collapse of the current administration in England led to Pitt's reappointment as prime minister. But illness kept him away from office for months at a time, and political battles and scheming made it impossible for him to forge an effective government. Weary and sick, he stepped down from office in November 1768.

By 1771, Pitt made only rare appearances in Parliament because of his poor health, but he remained concerned about the growing tensions between Britain and the American colonies. Pitt firmly supported British efforts to end the rebellion, and while he did not want to see the Americans gain total independence from Great Britain, he believed that they deserved to have greater control over their own futures. On April 7, 1778, he traveled to Parliament and delivered a speech in which he urged his countrymen to keep the British flag flying over the colonies. At the same time, he also asked Parliament to consider an arrangement in which the colonies would have significant powers of self-government, and he warned that it would be very difficult for Britain to win an all-out war with the Americans.

At the conclusion of this speech, Pitt collapsed. After undergoing medical treatment, he was taken back to his country estate, but he never regained his health. He remained confined to his bed for more than a month, and he died on May 11, 1778.

For More Information

Black, Jeremy. *Pitt the Elder.* New York: Cambridge University Press, 1992.

Encyclopedia of World Biography. Detroit: Gale, 1998.

Historic World Leaders. Reproduced in *Biography Resource Center.* Detroit: Gale Group, 2002.

Peters, Marie. *Pitt and Popularity: The Patriot Minister and London Opinion During the Seven Years War.* New York: Oxford University Press, 1980.

Pontiac

Born c. 1720
Great Lakes region

Died April 20, 1769
Cahokia, Illinois

Ottawa war chief who led a major Indian uprising against British forces

A chief of the Ottawa tribe, Pontiac is believed to have been one of the driving forces behind a massive Indian (Native American) rebellion waged against British forts and settlements from 1763 to 1765. This uprising—which came to be known as Pontiac's Rebellion—ranks as one of the greatest Indian alliances in North American history. During the course of this rebellion, which swept all along the western frontier, hundreds of white people were killed and several forts were captured. In addition, Pontiac personally led a band of warriors that nearly succeeded in taking Fort Detroit, the most important British outpost in the Great Lakes region. But his six-month siege of the fort ultimately failed, and in 1765, he agreed to lay down arms against the British soldiers and settlers that had moved into the region.

A chief of the powerful Ottawas

Little information on Pontiac's early life is known. Historians believe that he was the son of an Ottawa father and Ojibway mother, but they are not even sure of the year or

Ottawa tribe chief Pontiac.
Reproduced by permission of Getty Images.

place in which he was born. It is thought that he was born somewhere between 1718 and 1720, in one of three places within Ottawa territory: Michilimackinac, on the northern tip of Michigan's lower peninsula; along the Maumee River in modern-day Ohio; or along the Ottawa River near the Michigan-Ohio border.

Pontiac was tall and powerfully built, and he was evidently a strong warrior and leader, for Ottawa tribes selected their chiefs based on leadership and fighting skills as well as heredity. He may have had several wives and children, but historians are only aware of one wife—Kantuckeegan—and two sons.

Pontiac became a chief of the Ottawa nation at a time when tribes all around the Great Lakes had become dependent on trade with Frenchmen for their survival. For example, many Indians had become so reliant on rifles to hunt game and defend themselves from attack that they were no longer capable of using bows and arrows effectively. Other Indian traditions were also being lost because of the influence of the French traders. Still, the relationship between the Indian tribes and French traders and settlers was friendly and mutually respectful.

Not surprisingly, the Ottawas and many other Indian nations sided with the French when the French and Indian War (1754–63; known in Europe as the Seven Years' War) erupted. This war began in North America, where both Great Britain and France had established large colonies (permanent settlements of citizens who maintain ties to the mother country) throughout the eastern half of the continent. The British colonies, known as America, stretched along the Atlantic Ocean from present-day Maine to Georgia. The French colonies, known as New France, included eastern Canada, parts of the Great Lakes region, and the Mississippi River basin. Both the British and the French hoped to expand their land holdings into the Ohio Country, a vast wilderness that lay between their colonies. This region offered access to valuable natural resources and important river travel routes. But the Ohio Country was controlled by the Iroquois Confederacy, a powerful alliance of six Indian nations who had lived on the land for generations. When the influence of the Iroquois Confederacy began to decline in the mid-1700s, the British and French began fighting to claim the Ohio Country and take control of North America. Once Great Britain and France officially declared war in 1756, the conflict spread to Europe and around the world.

Pontiac's early encounters with the British

In 1759, British forces captured Quebec from the French. This victory marked the end of the war between French and British forces in North America. With Quebec in hand, British leaders sent Major **Robert Rogers** (1731–1795; see entry) and two hundred of his fellow American soldiers to accept the surrender of all French forts on the western frontier. As each commander surrendered, Rogers was expected to formally declare that the fort was now a part of the British Empire.

Rogers and his force began their journey in the fall of 1760, paddling across the Great Lakes in big whaleboats. One November evening, however, Rogers and his men were surrounded at their lakeshore camp by Pontiac and a large band of warriors. After talking with Rogers, Pontiac decided that he would attempt to live in peace with the British. Rogers and Pontiac took part in a peace pipe ceremony, and the Indian chief provided Rogers with protection from other Indian tribes as he continued his journey westward.

In the early 1760s, however, relations between the British and the Indian tribes became very tense. British military leaders issued orders prohibiting white men from selling ammunition, food, clothing, or alcohol to the Indians. Tribespeople were also turned away from forts and settlements they had visited for years. In the meantime, English farmers and hunters and tradesmen continued to build new houses and settlements in the region without regard for the feelings of the Indian nations that had long made their homes there. Pontiac reflected the sentiments of many Indians when he complained that the English were swarming into the Great Lakes region like mosquitoes in the swamps.

Pontiac and other Indian leaders recognized that the British were treating the tribes like trespassers on their own land. In addition, Pontiac and other Indians believed that the

French, with whom they had coexisted peacefully for years, might yet return. Pontiac thus devised a plan that called for all of the Indian tribes to unite and conquer all the British frontier forts at the same time. Pontiac thought that if the Indians seized the forts, they would be able to take ammunition, clothing, and other supplies they needed. More importantly, victories over the British might convince the French traders to return.

In 1762, Pontiac sent messengers to all of the region's tribal leaders, asking them to come to his village for a major conference. In April 1763, the tribal representatives gathered at Pontiac's camp near the shores of Lake Erie. Pontiac opened the war council by reminding his visitors of all the insults they had suffered at the hands of the British. He also recalled how the French had traded freely and fairly with the Indians. Finally, as noted in *Historic World Leaders,* Pontiac told them that the supreme god of the Indians wanted them to "lift the hatchet" against the British and renew their friendship with the French. But he added that the tribes should return to the traditions and lifestyles that they had followed before they met the white man. "You have bought guns, knives, kettles and blankets from the white men until you can no longer do without them; and, what is worse, you have drunk the poison firewater [alcohol], which turns you into fools," said Pontiac.

By the time the war council had concluded, sixteen Indian nations—including the Algonquins, the Hurons, the Senecas, and several tribes of the lower Mississippi—had agreed to join Pontiac's rebellion. A few weeks later, tribes across the west attacked forts and settlements that had been built in their midst. Eight of these forts eventually fell to their Indian attackers.

Pontiac attacks Fort Detroit

Pontiac's task in the uprising was to capture Fort Detroit, the biggest British fort in the Great Lakes Region. He settled on a scheme to enter the fort in a peaceful manner, then attack the soldiers within. But the commander of Fort Detroit, Major Henry Gladwin (1729–1791), learned that Pontiac planned to attack the outpost, and he was able to prepare for any trickery.

On May 7, 1763, Pontiac and forty warriors entered Fort Detroit, saying they wanted to meet with Gladwin. They were accompanied by hundreds of squaws (Indian women) and elders who had hidden guns and knives under their clothing. As Pontiac entered the fort, he expected the British soldiers inside to be relaxed and unprepared for any violence. But as he walked through the interior of the fort, he saw that heavily armed soldiers were all over the place, watching the Indians like hawks. As noted in *Historic World Leaders,* Gladwin later wrote that "they were so much surprised to see [our soldiers armed], that they could hardly sit down to council. However, in about half and hour, after they saw their designs [plans] were discovered, they sat down and Pontiac made a speech which I answered calmly, without intimating [showing] my suspicion of their intentions, and after receiving some trifling [small] presents, they went away to their camp."

Two days later, though, Pontiac returned with hundreds of warriors and laid siege to the fort. By surrounding the fort with his own men, the Ottawa chief hoped to prevent the 125 British soldiers inside from receiving food, ammunition, and other supplies. He believed the fort's defenders would surrender when they ran out of food and gunpowder. As the siege continued, Pontiac's men also attacked isolated white settlements in the region, killing some settlers and taking others captive.

As the weeks passed, Pontiac and his warriors intercepted a number of shipments of supplies that were intended for the fort. They also attacked soldiers sent to help defend the fort. They killed some soldiers on the field of battle, but others were captured and tortured before being put to death. Pontiac ordered many of these mutilated bodies to be thrown into the Detroit River, so they would float past Gladwin and the other British soldiers inside the fort.

In late July, however, nearly two dozen British boats carrying soldiers, cannons, ammunition, and other supplies slipped past Indian sentries in heavy fog and reached the fort. Captain James Dalyell (?–1763), a chief aide to General **Jeffery Amherst** (1717–1797; see entry), was part of this group. Soon after his arrival, he ordered a surprise nighttime raid on Pontiac's camp, which was about five miles away from the gates of the fort. But Pontiac learned of the plan, and he organized a brutal ambush of Dalyell's forces. A total of fifty-nine British soldiers were killed or wounded in the clash, and the troops were forced to flee back to the safety of the fort.

Throughout the summer of 1763, Pontiac expressed confidence that the French would return. But a trickle of supplies continued to make it to the fort, despite Pontiac's best efforts to cut off the flow. His frustration with the situation grew, and he reportedly subjected white captives to all sorts of torture and brutal treatment during this time. In late summer, Pontiac intercepted a message to Fort Detroit that stated that France and Great Britain had settled their differences with the Treaty of Paris. According to this agreement, the people of France acknowledged that all of the Great Lakes region was now British territory. But Pontiac's desire to see the French return was so great that he refused to believe the message.

Pontiac lifts the siege

In the fall, Pontiac's army began to fall apart. Some warriors drifted away to hunt for food that would sustain their families over the long winter. Others expressed doubt that the French would ever come to the Indians' aid. Around this same time, Pontiac received a letter from a French military commander on the Mississippi River. As noted in *Historic World Leaders,* the letter urged Pontiac and the other Indians to lay down their war hatchets "and live as brothers with the British.... Let there be peace in the Great Lakes!"

As autumn rolled across the Great Lakes, Pontiac finally admitted to himself that his bid to capture Fort Detroit had been unsuccessful. He also realized the massive Indian rebellion had failed to convince the French to resume hostilities against the British. On October 31, 1763, Pontiac lifted the six-month siege on Fort Detroit. He sent a note to Gladwin saying he wanted to have peaceful relations with the British. He then spent the winter in an Ottawa village on the Maumee River. In the spring of 1764, Pontiac tried to recruit warriors for another uprising. But this time, his words failed to generate any excitement, and an organized uprising never developed.

In August 1765, Pontiac finally agreed to stop fighting the British. In the spring of 1766, he signed a peace treaty in which he was pardoned (officially forgiven) for his role in the 1763 rebellion. He hoped that the agreement would convince the British to give gifts and supplies to the people of his tribe. But when these gifts failed to appear, his people rejected his chieftainship. He spent the next three years wandering the region, where he found that his reputation among the Ottawa and other tribes had declined dramatically. In fact, he became the target of ridicule by some of the younger warriors he encountered. He apparently engaged in no other violent acts against the British during this time.

In April 1769, Pontiac traveled to a trading post in Cahokia, Illinois, where he was killed under mysterious circumstances. Some accounts say that a Peoria Indian named Black Dog murdered him, possibly at the request of British leaders who still distrusted him. But other historians believe that he may have been killed by Indians angry about his decision to lay down arms against the British.

For More Information

Bland, Celia. *Pontiac: Ottawa Rebel.* New York: Chelsea House, 1995.

Dockstader, Frederick J. *Great North American Indians: Profiles in Life and Leadership.* New York: Van Nostrand Reinhold, 1977.

Encyclopedia of World Biography. Reproduced in *Biography Resource Center.* Detroit: Gale, 2002.

Fleischer, Jane. *Pontiac: Chief of the Ottawas.* Mahwah, NJ: Troll Associates, 1979.

Historic World Leaders. Detroit: Gale, 1994.

Notable Native Americans. Detroit: Gale, 1995.

Peckham, Howard H. *Pontiac and the Indian Uprising.* New York: Russell & Russell, 1970. Reprint, Detroit: Wayne State University Press, 1994.

Wheeler, Jill. *Forest Warrior: The Story of Pontiac.* Bloomington, IN: Abdo & Daughters, 1989.

Robert Rogers

Born November 7, 1731
Methuen, Massachusetts

Died May 18, 1795
London, England

American wilderness fighter, scout,
and leader of Rogers' Rangers

Robert Rogers. *Reproduced by permission of the Corbis Corporation.*

R obert Rogers was one of the most exciting figures to emerge during the French and Indian War (1754–63; known in Europe as the Seven Years' War). A rugged outdoorsman from the New Hampshire frontier, Rogers recruited other men like himself and formed companies of wilderness fighters known as Rogers' Rangers. The rangers provided valuable service to the British Army as scouts and raiders. In fact, they helped the British side in much the same way that Indian (Native American) allies helped the French side. Once the war ended, Rogers added to his fame by publishing his journals (see box), which are full of exciting tales about his wartime adventures.

Becomes a rugged frontiersman

Robert Rogers was born on November 7, 1731, in Methuen, Massachusetts Bay Colony. The son of James and Mary Rogers, Robert grew up on his family's farm near modern-day Concord, New Hampshire. During his youth, the area where he lived consisted mostly of wilderness, with a few small farms and villages scattered throughout. Since Rogers was needed to work on the farm, he received little formal education. As he grew older, he spent all his spare time in the wilderness—hunting, exploring, and trading with the Indians who lived there. By the time the French and Indian War broke out, Rogers had developed into a rugged frontiersman.

The French and Indian War began in 1754 in North America, where both Great Britain and France had established colonies (permanent settlements of citizens who maintain ties to the mother country). The British colonies, known as America, stretched along the Atlantic Ocean from present-day Maine to Georgia. The French colonies, known as New France, included eastern Canada, parts of the Great Lakes region, and the Mississippi River basin.

Both the British and the French hoped to expand their land holdings into the Ohio Country, a vast wilderness that lay between their colonies and offered access to valuable natural resources and important river travel routes. But the Ohio Country was controlled by the Iroquois Confederacy, a powerful alliance of six Indian nations whose members had lived on the land for generations. As Iroquois influence started to decline in the mid-1700s, however, the British and French began fighting to claim the Ohio Country and take control of North America. Once Great Britain and France officially declared war in 1756, the conflict spread to Europe and around the world.

In the early years of the French and Indian War, the French formed alliances with many Indian nations. The French and their Indian allies worked together to hand the British and their American colonists a series of defeats. Part of the reason for the French success was that they learned some of the Indians' methods of wilderness fighting. For example, they often hid in the woods and launched sneak attacks. In contrast, the British soldiers wore bright red uniforms and were trained to stand and fight in formation.

Leads wilderness fighters known as Rogers' Rangers

Rogers joined the army in 1755 and became a captain in the forces led by **William Johnson** (1715–1774; see entry).

In September of that year, Johnson led thirty-five hundred colonial troops and Indian warriors on a mission to attack Fort St. Frédéric, a French stronghold located on Lake Champlain in northern New York. Rogers used his wilderness experience and outdoor skills to scout enemy forces and gather information. He was also able to recruit and train other New Hampshire frontiersmen to perform this valuable service for Johnson's army. Although Johnson's forces did not capture Fort St. Frédéric, they did defeat the French and their Indian allies in the Battle of Lake George. This was the first important British victory of the war, and it also stopped the French from advancing further into New York.

In recognition of Rogers' talents, Johnson gave him command of his own unit of wilderness fighters—known as Rogers' Rangers—in 1756. Two years later, Rogers was promoted to the rank of major and placed in charge of nine ranger companies. The rangers were tough and hardy outdoorsmen who adopted the Indians' methods of wilderness warfare. For example, they learned skills like tracking, camouflage, signaling, and ambush.

Rogers came up with a detailed list of rules to guide the behavior of his rangers. The rangers wore dark green uniforms and black hats with a feather in them. They usually moved at night, under cover of darkness. They traveled across lakes in canoes or on ice skates, and they moved silently through the woods wearing moccasins or snowshoes. When they saw enemy forces, Rogers would give a hand signal that meant "tree all," and the rangers would disappear into the underbrush. Each ranger fought alongside a partner, so that one could shoot while the other reloaded his weapon. When the fighting became too intense, the rangers would scatter into the woods and regroup at a meeting place miles away.

Rogers' Rangers help the British war effort

Throughout the course of the war, Rogers' Rangers fought in a number of battles. In the early spring of 1758, for example, they scouted enemy forces near Fort Carillon. This French stronghold, known as Ticonderoga by the British, was

James Fenimore Cooper, Author of *Last of the Mohicans*

American author James Fenimore Cooper lived most of his life in the nineteenth century, but his most famous novel—*The Last of the Mohicans*—was set a century earlier, at the height of the French and Indian War.

Born September 15, 1789, in Burlington, New Jersey, Cooper was raised in wealthy surroundings. He spent most of his childhood in Cooperstown, New York, a settlement founded by his father, the prominent William Cooper (1754–1809). Here, William Cooper—a judge, real estate investor, and member of the U.S. House of Representatives—built a large family mansion to house his thirteen children. James and his brothers could often be found roaming the forests that surrounded the village, and it was these boyhood adventures that fueled Cooper's lifelong love for the outdoors.

Cooper was a reckless youth, and his wild behavior convinced Yale University administrators to expel him from the school in 1805. He then served for six years as a Merchant Marine (a sailor on a commercial ship) and as a sailor in the U.S. Navy before beginning a business career. In 1820, he began a long and successful writing career by publishing his first novel, titled *Precaution.* Over the next three decades, he wrote numerous novels, volumes of military history, and books of social criticism that made him one of the world's leading literary figures. The most famous of these works were his Leatherstocking Tales. These five novels—*The Pioneers* (1823), *The Last of the Mohicans* (1826), *The Prairie* (1827), *The Pathfinder* (1840), and *The Deerslayer* (1841)—told the story of a brave eighteenth-century frontiersman named Natty Bumppo, who was nicknamed Leatherstocking because of his clothing.

All five of Cooper's Leatherstocking books explored European settlers' brave struggles to develop the North American continent, as well as the unfortunate destruction of nature that accompanies such development. The most famous of the

located on Lake George in New York. British leaders were planning a major expedition against the fort that summer and sent Rogers and 180 rangers to gather information. But the French and their Indian allies knew the rangers were coming and set a trap for them. The rangers came upon a small group of Indians in the woods and started to chase them, when they suddenly ran into more than 500 Canadian and Indian forces. Rogers and his men made a fighting retreat, but dozens of rangers were killed or captured. Rogers himself escaped by sliding down a steep hill into the icy waters of the

James Fenimore Cooper. *Illustration by Cacilie Brandt. Reproduced by permission of the National Portrait Gallery, Smithsonian Institution.*

Leatherstocking tales is *Last of the Mohicans,* which describes Bumppo's adventures as a scout for the British during the French and Indian War. The novel follows Bumppo—nicknamed Hawkeye at this point in his life—as he and his noble Mohican Indian friends, Chingachook and Uncas, try to save the Munro sisters from the evil Magua and his fellow Iroquois warriors. *Last of the Mohicans* is marred by several historical inaccuracies, but it is also an exciting adventure tale that was hugely popular with critics and readers alike. Today, it remains the most widely read of Cooper's many stories, and Natty Bumppo continues to rank as "a character of genuine mythic proportions," according to the *Times Educational Supplement* (January 16, 1987, p. 32).

Later in his career, Cooper wrote works ranging from social criticism to nautical adventures about pirates and marooned sailors. These writings never achieved the popularity of his Natty Bumppo books, however. In the late 1840s, liver problems took a heavy toll on Cooper's health, and he died on September 14, 1851, just one day shy of his sixty-second birthday.

Source: Encyclopedia of World Biography.
Reproduced in Biography Resource Center. *Detroit: Gale, 2002.*

lake. Only 54 rangers made it back to their headquarters at Fort Edward.

British leaders also ordered Rogers and his rangers to conduct numerous raids against French forts and Indian villages. They made one of their most famous raids against the St. Francis Abenaki Indians in 1759. The Abenaki lived near the St. Lawrence River, between Montreal and Quebec. They were responsible for a series of bloody attacks that killed an estimated six hundred American colonists. Rogers and his

Excerpt from Rogers's Journal

The following passages are from Robert Rogers's account of the disastrous 1758 scouting mission against Fort Carillon, which took the lives of over one hundred rangers.

March 10, 1758. I was ordered by Col. [William] Haviland [the British commander of Fort Edward] to the neighbourhood of Ticonderoga [site of a French fort on Lake George], not with 400 men, as was at first given out, but with 180, officers included.... I acknowledge that I entered upon this service, with this small detachment [group] of brave men, with no small uneasiness of mind. We had every reason to believe that [a colonial soldier who had recently been taken prisoner by the French] had informed the enemy of our intended expedition, and the force to be employed....

[Rogers and his men left Fort Edward that day and started across the frozen surface of Lake George. When they neared Ticonderoga on March 13, they began moving through the woods on snowshoes.] On our left, at a small distance, we were flanked by a rivulet [stream], and by a steep mountain on the right. Our main body kept close under the mountain, that the advanced guard might better observe the brook, on the ice of which they might travel, as the snow was now four feet deep, which made the travelling very bad even with snow shoes. In this manner we proceeded a mile and a half, when our advance informed us that the enemy were in sight; and soon after, that his force consisted of ninety-six, chiefly Indians. We immediately threw down our knapsacks and prepared for battle, supposing that the whole of the enemy's force were approaching on our left, upon the ice of the rivulet.... We gave them the first fire, which killed more than forty and put the remainder to flight [caused them to retreat], in which one half of my men pursued, and cut down several more of them with their hatchets and cutlasses [short

rangers made a dangerous three-hundred-mile journey through enemy territory to attack the Abenaki. They killed up to two hundred Indians and burned the village to the ground.

Later in 1759, Rogers took part in the successful British attack on Fort St. Frédéric. The following year—just a few days after the French surrendered at Montreal—Rogers accepted the surrender of Fort Detroit to end the French and Indian War in North America. By this time, Rogers was famous throughout Great Britain and the American colonies. Stories of his courage and daring had made him a hero. In 1761, he married Elizabeth Browne, the daughter of a minister. Later that year, he took a company of rangers to South Carolina to help put down a Cherokee Indian uprising. In 1763, he fought in several battles against Indians during a large-scale rebellion led by an Ottawa chief named **Pontiac** (c. 1720–1769; see entry).

swords]. I now imagined they were totally defeated.... [But] the party we had routed was only the advanced guard of six hundred Canadians and Indians, who were now coming up to attack the Rangers. The latter now retreated to their own ground, which was gained at the expense of fifty men killed. There they were drawn up in good order, and fought with such intrepidity [courage], keeping up a constant and well directed fire, as caused the French, though [outnumbering the rangers by] seven to one in number, to retreat a second time. We however being in no condition to pursue, they rallied again, recovered their lost ground, and made a desperate attack upon our front, and wings....

[The enemy continued attacking and pushed the rangers up the mountainside.] A constant fire continued for an hour and a half, from the commencement [start] of the attack, during which time we lost eight officers and one hundred privates killed upon the spot. After doing all that brave men could do, the Rangers were compelled to break, each man looking out for himself....

[After spending two nights in the cold, the surviving rangers arrived back at Fort Edward on March 15.] I will not pretend to say what would have been the result of this unfortunate expedition, had our numbers been four hundred strong, as was contemplated [considered]; but it is due to those brave officers and men who accompanied me, most of whom are now no more, to declare that every man in his respective station [rank or position], behaved with uncommon resolution and coolness; nor do I recollect an instance, during the action, in which the prudence [judgment] or good conduct of one of them could be questioned.

Source: Rogers, Robert. Reminiscences of the French War: With Robert Rogers' Journal and a Memoir of General Stark. 3d ed. Freedom, NH: Freedom Historical Society, 1988.

Struggles with debts and illegal dealings

Once peace returned to North America, Rogers found himself without a way to earn a living. His debts mounted, and he got into trouble for trading illegally with Indians. In 1765, he moved to England in hopes of cashing in on his fame. During his years there, he published *Reminiscences of the French War,* a lively account of his wilderness battles that was drawn from his journals. He also published his views of the American colonies in *A Concise Account of North America.* Finally, he wrote *Ponteach, or the Savages of America: A Tragedy,* which was one of the first plays written by a native New Englander.

British leaders rewarded Rogers for his service by giving him command of Fort Michilimackinac, located in a remote region of Michigan. Rogers and his wife returned to

North America in 1767 and lived at this remote outpost on Lake Huron for two years. During this time, Rogers again found himself in trouble for trading illegally with the Indians. He returned to England in 1769 and struggled to make a living. Failure to pay his debts eventually landed him in prison, but his brother arranged his release.

Rogers returned to America in 1775, hoping to join the colonial army and fight in the American Revolution. But General **George Washington** (1732–1799; see entry) did not trust Rogers and refused to offer him a command. Rogers was put in prison as a suspected spy for the British the following year, but he escaped. He then openly supported the British side and recruited a company of wilderness fighters known as the Queen's American Rangers. He lost his command after suffering a defeat near White Plains, New York.

Rogers was divorced in 1778, and a short time later he was banished from New Hampshire. He fled to England in 1780, where he lived his last years in hardship and poverty. He died in a London boarding house on May 18, 1795. The rules that Rogers established for the conduct of his rangers are still studied and used today (in a modernized form) by the elite U.S. Army Rangers, known as the Green Berets.

For More Information

Cuneo, John R. *Robert Rogers of the Rangers*. New York: Oxford University Press, 1959. Reprint, Ticonderoga, NY: Fort Ticonderoga Museum, 1998.

Dictionary of American Biography. Reproduced in *Biography Resource Center*. Detroit: Gale, 2002.

"Robert Rogers." *History Detroit: 1701–2001*. http://www.historydetroit.com/people/robert_rogers.asp (accessed January 30, 2003).

"Rogers' Rangers." *Digital History Ltd.: The Gateway to the Past*. http://digitalhistory.org/rogers.html (accessed January 30, 2003).

Rogers, Robert. *Reminiscences of the French War: With Robert Rogers' Journal and a Memoir of General Stark*. 3d ed. Freedom, NH: Freedom Historical Society, 1988.

George Washington

Born February 22, 1732
Bridges Creek, Virginia

Died December 14, 1799
Mount Vernon, Virginia

American military leader who took part in early battles of the French and Indian War; later became first president of the United States

George Washington is one of the most famous figures in world history. As a young soldier in the French and Indian War (1754–63; known in Europe as the Seven Years' War), he was known throughout the American colonies for his bravery, fighting skills, and leadership abilities. His fame increased dramatically during the American Revolution, when he commanded all the colonies' armies. His guidance of the colonies' armed forces ultimately helped America gain its independence from Britain. Washington then agreed to serve two four-year terms as the first president of the United States. He guided the nation through its first uncertain years of existence, and in the process he helped lay the foundation for many of the nation's most important financial, legal, and political institutions.

French and Indian War brings trials and triumphs

George Washington was born and raised in a wealthy family of Virginia planters. Born on February 22, 1732, he

George Washington.
Courtesy of the Library of Congress.

was the oldest son of Augustine Washington, a plantation owner with significant land holdings, and his second wife, Mary Ball. Washington's father died when he was eleven years old. He spent his teen years living with his mother and other relatives, including a half-brother who lived at Mount Vernon, a prosperous family farm.

In 1749, Washington was named county surveyor, a position that called for him to travel deep into forests, meadows, and other sparsely populated areas to measure property boundaries. In 1752, he was named a major in the Virginia militia. One year later, the lieutenant governor of the Virginia colony, Robert Dinwiddie (1693–1770; see box in chapter 2), selected Washington for an important mission that would take him deep into the Ohio Country.

Over the previous few years, ownership of the Ohio Country region of North America had severely strained relations between the European powers of Great Britain and France. Both countries had already established large colonies (permanent settlements of citizens who maintain ties to the mother country) throughout the eastern half of the continent. The British colonies, known as America, stretched along the Atlantic Ocean from present-day Maine to Georgia. The French colonies, known as New France, included eastern Canada, parts of the Great Lakes region, and the Mississippi River basin. Both the British and French hoped to expand their land holdings into the Ohio Country, which lay between their colonies. This region offered access to valuable natural resources and important river travel routes. But the Ohio Country was controlled by the Iroquois Confederacy, a powerful alliance of six Indian (Native American) nations who had lived on the land for generations. When the influence of the Iroquois Confederacy began to decline in the mid-1700s, the British and French began maneuvering to claim the region for themselves.

Washington's mission was to travel through the vast wilderness of the Ohio Valley and tell French officials that they were trespassing on British land. Washington and a small band of soldiers set out for the Ohio Country in October 1753. Braving cold weather and deep forests that lacked trails, Washington delivered his message to the French, who were building a number of forts in the region. But the French rejected Britain's claim that it owned the land, and Washington barely survived the dangerous winter journey back to Virginia. The following year, Washington's widely published account of his experiences in the wilderness (see box in chapter 2) made him famous throughout the colonies.

Washington's second campaign into the Ohio Country

In 1754, Washington was promoted to lieutenant colonel and sent back into the Ohio Country with two hundred soldiers. This expedition was not successful, however. His army was too small to seize Fort Duquesne, a French stronghold located on the banks of the Ohio River. He also clashed with French troops near an area called Red Stone Fort on May 28. Washington's force won the skirmish and captured several French soldiers, including a young officer named Joseph Coulon de Villiers de Jumonville (1718–1754). But an Indian chief named Tanaghrisson (?–1754; see box in chapter 3), who had helped Washington track the French, murdered Jumonville without warning. Tanaghrisson's warriors then turned on several other French prisoners and killed them. Washington was shocked by the sudden turn of events. He set out for home with his army, but French troops based at Fort Duquesne gave chase, joined by their Indian allies. The French surrounded Washington's exhausted troops at a makeshift outpost called Fort Necessity. But since war had not formally been declared between France and Great Britain, the French commander was not sure that he could take Washington and his men prisoner. He eventually decided to let them go after Washington signed a document in which he accepted responsibility for the death of Jumonville.

A disheartened Washington and his troops returned to Virginia. But as it turned out, his clashes with the French—and his admission that Jumonville had been killed while in his custody—brought the simmering hostilities between France and Great Britain to a boil. In 1755, a British effort to push the French out of the Ohio Country ended in humiliating defeat, and one year later the two nations formally declared war against one another for control of North America.

In July 1754, Colonel George Washington signs a document at Fort Necessity accepting responsibility for the death of French officer Joseph Coulon de Villiers de Jumonville. *Reproduced by permission of Getty Images.*

Washington had served as a military aide to General **Edward Braddock** (1695–1755; see entry) on the disastrous British military campaign of 1755. In fact, he was one of the few British and colonial officers to escape without injury, despite his courageous action during the fighting. But after the French and Indian War formally erupted in 1756, he participated in no more assaults against the French. Instead, he was charged with helping English frontier settlements improve their defenses against Indian attacks.

One of Virginia's leading citizens

In 1758, Washington was elected to the Virginia House of Burgesses (a representative body made up of Virginia colonists but under the authority of British rule). For the remainder of the French and Indian War, he divided his time between legislative duties, service as a county judge, and supervision of the large family farms he owned. On January 6, 1759, he married a widow named Martha Dandridge Custis, and settled down with her on the family estate at Mount Vernon.

From 1760 to 1775, Washington tirelessly tended his many farm operations, but he also remained one of the colonies' most visible legislators. During this period, he and many other Americans became very angry about British policies toward the colonies. Washington and countless other colonists believed they needed to be independent from Great Britain in order to create a free and democratic society. In 1775, the differences between the British and the Americans finally erupted into war. America's First Continental Congress—a group of representatives from all of the colonies—unanimously selected Washington to command the colonies in their bid to gain independence. The Virginian was chosen not only because of his reputation for bravery and honesty, but also because of his knowledge of the British military. In addition, Washington's southern background helped address the concerns of some Americans that the northern colonies of New England were pushing all the colonies into war.

Commander of the colonial army

When Washington agreed to lead the colonial army, he privately wondered if he was up to the task. After all, he not only had to create, train, and outfit an army within a matter of months, but he also had to make it effective enough to stand against British military forces that ranked as the most powerful in the world.

The first few years of the Revolutionary War (1775–83) against the British were very difficult for Washington and his army. Hampered by serious supply shortages, officers with limited experience, and American colonists who wished to remain part of the British Empire, the colonial forces barely survived. But Washington's troops developed a deep loyalty to their commander and their cause, and the Virginian gained a deep respect for his soldiers as well. In 1778, for example, as noted in *The Writings of George Washington,* he wrote that "to see men without clothes to cover their nakedness, without blankets to lay on, without shoes, by which their marches may be traced by the blood from their feet, and almost as often without provisions as with, marching through frost and snow ... is a mark of patience and obedience which ... can scarce be paralleled."

As the War for Independence progressed, Washington directed the American war effort with mixed success. In six of the nine battles in which he personally fought, his forces either lost or could claim no better than a draw. But Washington also delivered major victories over the British at Trenton, Harlem Heights, and Yorktown, and he captured Boston from the British when he threatened to hammer it with cannons. These triumphs convinced foreign countries—such as France—to provide badly needed assistance to the American cause. In addition, Washington refused to steal supplies or take advantage of local communities, no matter how desperate his situation became. By conducting the war in this way, he kept the support of the American people throughout the long conflict.

In 1783, Great Britain finally gave up on its grim struggle to keep the American colonies loyal to the British Crown. The colonies were now free to create their own government, which Washington hoped would be formed with an eye toward ensuring that "our lives, liberties and properties shall be preserved."

On December 23, 1783, Washington resigned his position as commander of America's armed forces and headed home to Mount Vernon. He arrived at his farm on Christmas Eve, grateful to return to the life of a farmer. But before long, the newly formed nation he had helped create called on him once again.

First president of the United States

In 1787, leading citizens from across the United States gathered in Philadelphia, Pennsylvania, at a Constitutional

Convention. This meeting produced the Constitution of the United States—still the cornerstone of America's legal system—and outlined the type of government under which Americans would live. At this same meeting, the delegates unanimously selected Washington to be the first president of the United States.

Washington was inaugurated as president of the United States of America in New York City on April 30, 1789. He knew that his actions and behavior would shape the country—and the role of the presidency—for generations to come. With this in mind, he paid special attention to behaving in an honorable and truthful fashion at all times. As noted in *The Writings of George Washington,* the president declared, "I hope I shall always possess firmness and virtue enough to maintain the character of an honest man, as well as prove that I am [an honest man]."

In 1790, Washington came down with pneumonia. As he fought against the illness, the entire nation expressed concern that their fragile nation might fall apart if he died. After all, no other figure was as universally loved and respected as this Revolutionary War hero. "You cannot conceive the public alarm [at his sickness]," wrote Washington's secretary of state, Thomas Jefferson (1743–1826), to a friend. "It proves how much depends on his life."

Washington recovered, and during his first four years in office he oversaw many significant accomplishments. He established a philosophy of strong national government, helped create the federal court system, and oversaw the development of a monetary system that soon made the United States an international economic power.

Washington wanted to retire to his farm at Mount Vernon after concluding his first four-year term. But the country's leading legislators and political leaders begged him to reconsider. They recognized that the United States was still in a fragile state. Most lawmakers and citizens had divided into separate political camps that wanted to take the country in different directions. Many Americans worried that without Washington's leadership, the bitter disputes between the political parties might tear apart the country.

Washington reluctantly agreed to a second term, and in 1792, he was unanimously reelected. His second four-year term was a difficult one in several respects. In 1794, he was forced to use military power to end the so-called Whiskey Rebellion—a protest by farmers against a federal tax on whiskey. In addition, he was forced to devote much of his attention to diplomatic maneuvers to avoid being dragged into another war that had flared up between France and Great Britain. Washington strongly believed that the United States, which was still struggling to establish itself, could not afford to be drawn into an expensive war.

As the conclusion of Washington's second term drew near, the nation's first president opted against running for a third time. So in March 1797, Washington's presidential tenure ended, and he peacefully handed over the office to John Adams (1735–1826), who had been Washington's vice president for both terms. Washington went home to Mount Vernon, where he resumed the life of a wealthy farmer. In 1798, the threat of a French invasion nearly returned Washington to the role of general of the American army. But the United States and France settled their differences without violence, and Washington remained in Virginia.

On December 14, 1799, George Washington died from a throat infection that struck him down with stunning suddenness. News of his death shocked the United States and the rest of the world. By this time, the country that he had helped bring into existence was able to survive the blow. But the loss of Washington, who, by now, was known throughout the United States as "the father of our country," still prompted heartfelt tributes and testimonials in cities and villages across America.

For More Information

Alden, John R. *George Washington: A Biography.* Baton Rouge: Louisiana State University Press, 1984. Reprint, New York: Wings Books, 1995.

Encyclopedia of World Biography. Reproduced in *Biography Resource Center.* Detroit: Gale, 2002.

Fitzpatrick, John C., ed. *The Writings of George Washington from the Original Manuscript Sources, 1745–1799.* 39 vols. Washington: U.S. Govt. Print. Office, 1931–44. Reprint, Westport, CT: Greenwood Press, 1970.

Jones, Robert F. *George Washington.* Rev. ed. New York: Fordham University Press, 1986.

Marrin, Albert. *George Washington and the Founding of a Nation.* New York: Dutton Children's Books, 2001.

McClung, Robert M. *Young George Washington and the French and Indian War, 1753–1758.* North Haven, CT: Linnet Books, 2002.

Meltzer, Milton. *George Washington and the Birth of Our Nation.* New York: F. Watts, 1986.

Randall, Willard S. *George Washington: A Life.* New York: Henry Holt & Co., 1997.

Spalding, Matthew, and Patrick J. Garrity. *A Sacred Union of Citizens: George Washington's Farewell Address and the American Character.* Lanham, MD: Rowman & Littlefield, 1996.

Wall, Charles Cecil. *George Washington, Citizen-Soldier.* Charlottesville: University Press of Virginia, 1980.

James Wolfe

Born January 2, 1727
Westerhan, Kent, England

Died September 13, 1759
Quebec, Canada

British general who led the capture of Quebec

James Wolfe. *Courtesy of the Library of Congress.*

James Wolfe was a hero for the British during the French and Indian War. After playing an important role in the successful siege of Louisbourg in 1758, he was promoted to the rank of major general and given command of the British attack on Quebec in 1759. Wolfe tried a number of different strategies to capture the fortress city on a cliff. He finally discovered an overgrown footpath that allowed his troops to move onto the plains behind the city. His British forces defeated the French there in one of the most pivotal battles of the war.

A rising young officer

James Wolfe was born on January 2, 1727, in Westerhan, Kent, England. Both his father and grandfather had served in the British Army, and James grew up wanting a military career. He joined his father's unit at the age of thirteen, and two years later he received a commission as an officer. In 1742, he transferred to the Twelfth Regiment of Foot. Wolfe fought in Europe during the War of the Austrian Succession (1744-48; also known as King George's War). He saw action in several important battles. In fact, one of Great Britain's top military leaders, William Augustus, the duke of Cumberland (1721–1765), praised his performance in the Battle of Lanfoldt. In 1750, at the age of twenty-three, Wolfe was promoted to the rank of lieutenant colonel and given command of a regiment.

Wolfe was a rising young officer when the French and Indian War (1754–63; known in Europe as the Seven Years' War) broke out. This conflict began in North America, where both Great Britain and France had established colonies (permanent settlements of citizens who maintain ties to the mother country). The British colonies, known as America, stretched along the Atlantic Ocean from present-day Maine to Georgia. The French colonies, known as New France, included eastern Canada, parts of the Great Lakes region, and the Mississippi River basin.

Both the British and the French hoped to expand their land holdings into the Ohio Country, a vast wilderness that lay between their colonies and offered access to valuable natural resources and important river travel routes. But the Ohio Country was controlled by the Iroquois Confederacy, a powerful alliance of six Indian (Native American) nations whose members had lived on the land for generations. As Iroquois influence started to decline in the mid-1700s, however, the British and French began fighting to claim the Ohio Country and take control of North America. Once Great Britain and France officially declared war in 1756, the conflict spread to Europe and around the world.

In the early years of the French and Indian War, the French formed alliances with many Indian nations. The French and their Indian allies worked together to hand the British and their American colonists a series of defeats. In 1757, however, **William Pitt** (1708–1788; see entry) became secretary of state in the British government and took charge of the British war effort. Pitt felt that the key to defeating France was to attack French colonies around the world. He decided to send thousands of British troops to North America and launch an invasion of Canada. Like other British leaders, Pitt was frustrated by the British Army's lack of success in North America. He believed that part of the problem was a lack of strong leadership. When Pitt asked his top military leaders for the names of talented young officers to direct the war in North America, one of them recommended Wolfe.

Plays an important role in the capture of Louisbourg

Wolfe traveled to North America in 1758. He served as a brigade commander under General **Jeffery Amherst** (1717–1797; see entry) during the siege of Louisbourg. Louisbourg was a fortress city on Cape Breton Island, off the Atlantic Coast of Canada, that guarded the entrance to the St. Lawrence River. Amherst brought twelve thousand British troops up the coast by ship in early June. Wolfe led the first group of soldiers to shore. After a rough landing, they came under fire from French forces, but eventually managed to secure the beach. Then the British troops hauled artillery on shore to set up a siege (a military strategy that involves surrounding a target, cutting it off from outside help and supplies, and using artillery to break down its defenses).

Amherst's forces surrounded the city by early July and began pounding it with artillery fire. The British finally broke through Louisbourg's defenses and forced the city to surrender on July 26. The capture of Louisbourg gave the British a clear path up the St. Lawrence River to attack the important French cities of Quebec and Montreal. Controlling Louisbourg also helped them to prevent French ships from bringing fresh troops and supplies to Canada.

Wolfe returned to England following the successful capture of Louisbourg, at which time Pitt promoted him to the rank of major general and gave him command of a military campaign against Quebec that was planned for 1759. Since Wolfe was only thirty-two years old at this time, many older officers were insulted that he received such an important command. In fact, some of these officers spread rumors that Wolfe was insane. But King George II (1683–1760) remembered the defeats that his forces had suffered early in the war. He was ready to make a change in leadership in the North American war effort. "Mad is he?" the king replied upon hearing the rumors about Wolfe. "Then I hope he'll bite some of my other generals."

In fact, Wolfe was an unusual character. He was tall and thin with bright red hair. He suffered from poor health throughout his life and once described himself as a "skeleton in motion." Wolfe was highly emotional and had a quick temper, which sometimes earned him enemies. He also had a passion for learning that led him to hire tutors in Latin and mathematics and to read countless books about warfare. As a general, Wolfe believed in developing his own methods of doing things and often ignored the strict rules of the British Army. For example, he allowed his troops to wear more comfortable uniforms and outlawed whipping as a punishment. He also liked to recite poetry to his troops before going into battle. Although his men did not always like him, they did respect him.

Leads the British attack on Quebec

A fleet of British warships set sail up the St. Lawrence River from Louisbourg and arrived in Quebec in late June 1759. These ships carried Wolfe and more than eight thousand British troops under his command. When Wolfe got his first glimpse of Quebec, he worried that they were about to attack "the strongest country in the world." The capital of New France sat atop high cliffs overlooking the St. Lawrence River, and was surrounded by a large stone wall. The French commander, **Louis-Joseph, marquis de Montcalm-Gozon de Saint-Véran** (1712–1759; see entry), had placed two thousand French soldiers within the walls of the city and arranged his remaining twelve thousand troops along the bank of the St. Lawrence. The French defensive line stretched along the cliffs east of the city for seven miles, between the St. Charles and Montmorency Rivers.

Wolfe set up a base camp on the Île d'Orléans, a large island in the middle of the St. Lawrence, just a few miles from the city. Over the next two months, the British forces made several attempts to break through the French defensive line. On July 9, Wolfe ordered an attack on the east side of the French line, near the Montmorency River, but the British troops were turned back by heavy French gunfire. On July 12, the British forces began firing artillery shells into the city from Point Levis, a tall cliff directly across the river from Quebec. On July 31, Wolfe ordered another attack on the French lines below the city. But time after time, Montcalm's forces held off the attacks and refused to be drawn out of their strategic positions.

As the summer passed, Wolfe grew more and more frustrated at his inability to land troops on shore and set up a siege of Quebec. He knew that time was on the side of the French. At the first hint of winter, the British fleet would be forced to withdraw from the St. Lawrence, ending the expedition. Another factor in Wolfe's frustration was his declining health. He suffered from painful kidney stones, as well as a terrible fever and cough. As he grew weaker, Wolfe became convinced that he was going to die. He decided that he would rather die a glorious death on the field of battle than die slowly from disease.

Dies a hero

Desperate to earn a reputation as a brilliant general before he died, Wolfe began planning a final attack on the French lines. This time, the British troops would attempt to land west of Quebec at a spot called L'Anse au Foulon, which later became known as Wolfe's Cove. An overgrown footpath led from the cove to the top of the cliffs a short distance up-river from the city. This path could give the British access to the Plains of Abraham, broad fields that stretched behind Quebec and provided an ideal place to set up a siege.

On the night of September 12, a few British soldiers scrambled up the path to the top of the cliff and overpowered a small group of French guards. Wolfe followed with five thousand British troops, which he arranged in battle formation on the Plains of Abraham. Montcalm decided to engage the British forces in battle before they had a chance to dig trenches and set up a siege. The French general led an army of forty-five hundred troops across the Plains to begin the battle. Wolfe's forces stood their ground and waited until the enemy came within firing range. Then the British opened fire and devastated the French troops. Montcalm and most of his officers were killed, and around fourteen hundred French soldiers were killed or wounded. The inexperienced French troops then turned around and fled back toward the walls of the city.

Wolfe received wounds to the wrist and the abdomen early in the battle, but he stayed on his horse and continued to give orders to his troops. As the French forces began to retreat, however, the British general was shot through the lungs. He died a short time later, although he lived long enough to know that he had won the battle. "Now, God be praised," he said as he died. "Since I have conquered, I will die in peace." Wolfe's body was returned to England, where he received a hero's funeral. He was buried in a family vault at Greenwich. Meanwhile, Quebec surrendered to the British on September 18. Wolfe's victory reduced French territory in North America to Montreal and a few forts along the Great Lakes. Montreal surrendered to British forces in 1760 in America to end the French and Indian War and give the British control over all French territory in North America.

For More Information

Encyclopedia of World Biography. Detroit: Gale, 1998.

Garrett, Richard. *General Wolfe.* London: Barker, 1975.

Hibbert, Christopher. *Wolfe at Quebec.* Cleveland: World Pub. Co., 1959. Reprint, New York: Cooper Square Press, 1999.

Lloyd, Christopher. *The Capture of Quebec.* New York: Macmillan, 1959.

Parkman, Francis. *Montcalm and Wolfe.* Boston: Little, Brown and Company, 1884. Reprint, New York: Modern Library, 1999.

Reilly, Robin. *Wolfe of Quebec.* London: Cassell, 2001.

Whitton, Frederick. *Wolfe and North America.* Port Washington, NY: Kennikat Press, 1971.

Where to Learn More

Books

Anderson, Fred. *Crucible of War: The Seven Years' War and the Fate of Empire in British North America, 1754–1766.* New York: Knopf, 2000.

Carter, Alden R. *The Colonial Wars: Clashes in the Wilderness.* New York: Franklin Watts, 1992.

Chidsey, Donald Barr. *The French and Indian War: An Informal History.* New York: Crown, 1969.

Collier, Christopher, and James Lincoln Collier. *The French and Indian War, 1660–1763.* New York: Benchmark Books, 1998.

Hamilton, Edward P. *The French and Indian Wars: The Story of Battles and Forts in the Wilderness.* Garden City, NY: Doubleday, 1962.

Jennings, Francis. *Empire of Fortune: Crowns, Colonies, and Tribes in the Seven Years War in America.* New York: Norton, 1988.

Kopperman, Paul E. *Braddock at the Monongahela.* Pittsburgh: University of Pittsburgh Press, 1977.

Leckie, Robert. *"A Few Acres of Snow": The Saga of the French and Indian Wars.* New York: Wiley, 1999.

Marrin, Albert. *Struggle for a Continent: The French and Indian Wars, 1690–1760.* New York: Atheneum, 1987.

Minks, Benton, and Louise Minks. *The French and Indian War.* San Diego: Lucent Books, 1995.

O'Meara, Walter. *Guns at the Forks*. Englewood Cliffs, NJ: Prentice-Hall, 1965. Reprint, Pittsburgh: University of Pittsburgh Press, 1979.

Schwartz, Seymour I. *The French and Indian War, 1754–1763: The Imperial Struggle for North America*. New York: Simon and Schuster, 1994.

Web Sites of Selected French and Indian War Forts

Fort Beauséjour. http://www.fortbeausejour.com/ (accessed February 7, 2003).

Fort Frederick State Park. http://www.dnr.state.md.us/publiclands/western/fortfrederick.html (accessed February 6, 2003).

Fort Necessity National Battlefield. http://www.nps.gov/fone/home.htm (accessed February 6, 2003).

Fort Pitt Museum & Bushy Run Battlefield. http://www.fortpittmuseum.com/ (accessed February 6, 2003).

Fort Ticonderoga National Historic Landmark. http://www.fort-ticonderoga.org/ (accessed February 7, 2003).

The Fortress of Louisbourg. http://www.louisbourg.ca/fort/ (accessed February 6, 2003).

The "Official" Web Site of Old Fort Niagara. http://www.oldfortniagara.org/ (accessed February 7, 2003).

Index

Bold type indicates biography entries and their page numbers. Illustrations are marked by (ill.).